THE ALMANAC OF QUOTABLE QUOTES
FROM 1990

Ronald D. Pasquariello

PRENTICE HALL
Englewood Cliffs, New Jersey 07632

Prentice-Hall International (UK) Limited, *London*
Prentice-Hall of Australia Pty. Limited, *Sydney*
Prentice-Hall Canada, Inc., *Toronto*
Prentice-Hall Hispanoamericana, S.A., *Mexico*
Prentice-Hall of India Private Limited, *New Delhi*
Prentice-Hall of Japan, Inc., *Tokyo*
Simon & Schuster Asia Pte. Ltd., *Singapore*
Editora Prentice-Hall do Brasil, Ltda., *Rio de Janeiro*

1991 *by*

Ronald D. Pasquariello

10 9 8 7 6 5 4 3 2 1

Library of Congress Cataloging-in-Publication Data

The Almanac of quotable quotes from 1990 / [compiled] by Ronald D. Pasquariello.
    p. cm.
  Includes index.
  ISBN 0-13-026386-9 (case) ISBN 0-13-026378-8 (paper)
  1. Quotations. I. Pasquariello, Ronald D.
PN6081.A54   1991
081–dc20   90-25345
                                              CIP

ISBN 0-13-026386-9

ISBN 0-13-026378-8 (PBK)

PRENTICE HALL
BUSINESS & PROFESSIONAL DIVISION
A division of Simon & Schuster
Englewood Cliffs, New Jersey 07632

Printed in the United States of America

In memory of
David Marsh Barton,
"the last elegant bear."
Gentle, he made a difference.

Introduction

From Wall Street to Rodeo Drive, from the White House to the Kremlin, from "Roseanne" to "Sixty Minutes," from Yankee Stadium to Neiman Marcus, from Oleg Cassini to Levis, from 2 Live Crew to Dan Quayle, from "The Simpsons" to the First Family, *The Almanac of Quotable Quotes from 1990* is a sometimes serious, sometimes hilarious, and always entertaining look at 1990 in review.

This annual review is unique, because it is not by some pipe-puffing or perfumed pedant discoursing on the hidden meanings of recent events. No, *The Almanac of Quotable Quotes from 1990* is simply *"We by Us."* It collects what "We" said about "Us," what the person in the street or in the movie studio, or in the White House, or in the town squares of Eastern Europe, or on the playing fields, or in the polling places had to say about the people and events of the past year. The authors of this book are many. It is not mine, but ours.

What qualified a quotation to get into this book? It simply had to be a verbalization that was made in 1990.

It didn't have to be a quote of the type you might find in a venerable and familiar collection like *Bartlett's*. It didn't even have to be a complete sentence (forgive us, Mrs. Grundy) to merit inclusion. It could be something from a T-shirt, or a bumper sticker. A name, if it were for a new 1990 invention or product, would do, as well as the conclusions from some study or poll—any word or collection of them, as long as they met the primary directive: to reflect what we were or thought we were in 1990.

You won't find here, for example, Kennedy's "Ask not what your country can do for you...," or Lincoln's "A Government of the people, by the people...," or something from Socrates, Sojourner Truth, Buddha or, heck, Marilyn Monroe.

What you will find are what Barbara as well as George Bush had to say about things, what Madonna had to say about *Dick*

Tracy costar, Warren Beatty, what José Canseco and Joe Montana had to say about their most intense moments of concentration at bat or in the pocket. You'll also get *public* reaction to, for example, George Bush's change of (lip) position on his promise not to raise taxes, or to the ongoing abortion debate, or to wrongs in the animal rights controversy, or to the rise in crime.

You'll hear about what men and women think of each other (which will lead you to wonder how the species has managed to survive), and what our favorite flavor of ice cream is. You'll find out how much we're paying CEOs and how much we're paying security guards (just about a three-zero difference).

When this book was designed, I thought restricting it to one year would make it one of the thinnest books of the year. After all, how often would something witty or wise, or silly or stupid, be said? And what were my chances of discovering it once said?

The pages that follow are evidence that I grossly underestimated the oral genius of the American people. At a moment's notice, with the merest flick of a lip, we can be intriguing, profound, moving, insightful, amusing, clever, or outrageous. Off the cuff or on, our statements are pithy and well-said. They are gems of brevity, wit, and originality.

Letters to the editor are filled with the same kind of *mots justes* or *bon mots* that we have come to expect from the well-paid likes of Erma Bombeck, Bill Safire, Calvin Trilling, Russell Baker, and Nora Ephron. Person-in-the-street interviews are often wiser than the sages-of-the-moment who appear on "The MacNeill-Lehrer Report" or "Nightline."

One of the most difficult chapters, I had anticipated, would be the last, "Far Out," which was to be a collection of the dumb or embarrassing (to the listener, if not to the speaker) things we say. I discovered, instead, that there are more Americans walking around with their foot in their mouth than the size of podiatry's clientele would lead you to believe. Sexism, in particular, is rampant. But it appears to be an equal opportunity inf(l)ection—prevalent among both sexes.

The phrases you find in this book will be trivial, shallow, foolish, and ponderous, or wise, profound, eloquent, and generous. Sometimes they disclose how things really work; sometimes they insightfully describe the basic principles or ideas by which we live. Sometimes they reveal "Us" to ourselves quite vividly; sometimes they let us in on the thinking that went into the momentous decisions that changed our lives.

The Almanac of Quotable Quotes from 1990 is a verbal history of the year, a collage of living ideas from the twelve months that we called 1990, a rich panorama of the way we viewed the year as we were experiencing it, a recapping of major events, ideas, and personalities of the year.

The Almanac of Quotable Quotes from 1990 is an instant replay of the year gone by. It will give the reader another look at 1990 from a different angle—through the eyes and words of its players. With each turn of the page, the reader will relive—sometimes with a chuckle, sometimes with a chill, sometimes with a cry— the events and experiences that shaped "Us" in 1990.

You would think that someone who has had the opportunity I had to survey the year and to gather together the pieces of what we thought of it could easily come up with a pithy phrase to title it, like "Naughty Ninety," or "Nifty Ninety." Actually, I hammered my brain (which may well be the cause of the problem), and I've come up with nothing cute.

President Bush did make a poignant remark that might do. Reflecting, after his summit with Gorbachev, on the realignment of the superpowers that was brought to focus by the Iraqi invasion of Kuwait, he said that this might be "the beginning of a new world order." That is very well what 1990 may prove to be, in the aftermath of *perestroika*, the first year of a new world order. Let's hope.

Readers who wish to submit quotations for inclusion in the 1991 edition of Almanac of Quotable Quotes, please send a tear sheet or photocopy to Ronald D. Pasquariello, 2261 Market Street, Box 295, San Francisco, CA 94114.

Contents

Chapter 1

PEOPLE

GEORGE BUSH

We must unleash the resources of the profit and non-profit sectors, of the churches and synagogues, states and localities in our great national enterprise to assure safe, decent, and affordable housing for all . . . Only then will we be able to complete our vision of a free and prosperous America full of opportunity for people everywhere.

President George Bush

People understand that Congress bears a greater responsibility for this. But I'm not trying to assign blame.

President George Bush

Bush is basically a decent man whose decency, unfortunately, is about an eighth of an inch thick . . . he can be had cheap—political convenience will certainly suffice.

Columnist Michael Kinsley

George Bush's great good fortune is that he is a man utterly incapable of vision at a time when the people do not want vision and do not need it.

Columnist Charles Krauthammer

My mother made me eat it. And I'm President of the U.S., and I'm not going to eat any more broccoli.

President George Bush

Broccoli is higher in nutrients than almost any other vegetable.

According to TUFTS UNIVERSITY DIET & NUTRITION LETTER

I have not ordered it off Air Force One. I have just said, "don't you dare bring me another sprig of that vegetable."

President George Bush

The President simply hates broccoli.

White House statement

The gap between [President] Bush's own rhetoric and his resolve is awesome.

Columnist David S. Broder

[George] Bush does not give speeches. He gives remarks.

An anonymous administration official

We'd get along just fine with the Chinese students if they'd learn not to question our authority and behave toward us in a friendly and docile manner . . . like Bush and the Senate!

Chinese leaders according to cartoonist Mike Luckovich

DAN QUAYLE

Mars is essentially in the same orbit. Mars is somewhat the same distance from the sun, which is very important. We have seen pictures where there are canals, we believe, and water. If there is water, that means there is oxygen. If oxygen, that means we can breathe.

Vice President Dan Quayle

[The Soviet Union] subsidized Cuba to the tune of $5 billion a year. It's too bad they couldn't take the $5 billion and put it for housing in the Soviet Union or perhaps get better food service for the people in the Soviet Union.

Vice President Dan Quayle

I just don't think we ought to look for radical changes in our defense spending posture. The dividend of peace is peace. We've invested in national security and we got peace.

Vice President Dan Quayle

While the Soviet Union should not threaten Lithuania, if the Soviet Union is applying disciplinary measures to people in their own military, that's a different situation.

Vice President Dan Quayle

I believe we are on an irreversible trend toward more freedom and democracy—but that could change.

Vice President Dan Quayle as quoted by Anita Katz

Dan Quayle seems to be doing his job—making Bush look smart and presidential by comparison.

Anita Katz

You have to keep making fun of Dan Quayle, because as soon as we let up on him he'll be taken seriously and then he could be elected.

Author Paul Slansky

For love of country keep George healthy!

Bumper sticker

Thank God somebody is keeping an eye on our beloved Vice President lest he slip into oblivion and turn up as our President one fateful day.

Chris Stangel

Dan Quayle: Underachiever and proud of it, man?

T shirt

You must admit our President is no dummy. So why did he choose Dan Quayle to be his Vice President? Mr. Bush must have seen and known something that some of the people, like you, didn't know about.

Genevieve Irons

Quayle gave President Bush a present—a toilet paper holder that plays "Hail to the Chief."

According to WASHINGTONIAN

I think you should give Dan Quayle credit for persistence. He has reportedly learned to spell SUNUNU by practicing with a banana.

Tom Page

I haven't changed my views. I just hadn't anticipated that Dan Quayle would become my spokesman.

From a cartoon by Stevenson

I feel that Mr. Quayle gives us all we hope—after all, he demonstrates graphically that truth of the old saying that in America anyone can become Vice President.

Keith H. Johnson

In my view, Dan Quayle will be on the ticket [in 1992], not just because George Bush is loyal, which he is perhaps to a fault, but because he will not be a liability by the time the next election rolls around.

Richard Nixon

I looked into those blue eyes, and I might as well have been looking out the window.

William Cnaugh, V.P. Dan Quayle's college professor

Quayle was born not only roughly a quarter-century after any preceding President; he spent another quarter-century blissfully AWOL from history.

Garry Wills

For all the jokes, we must take Dan Quayle seriously. We must do so, because Bush did not.

Garry Wills

I doubt that Quayle is more lecherous than Kennedy, more crooked than Johnson, more unprincipled than Nixon, more ineffectual than Ford or Carter, more hypocritical than Reagan or Bush, more venal than Congress, less bound by the Constitution than the federal judiciary, more arrogant than the bureaucracy or more apathetic than the electorate. I am less concerned with Quayle's qualifications than I am with the continued viability of our democracy.

Kenneth E. Runyon

If a tree fell in a forest, and no one was there to hear it, it might sound like Dan Quayle looks.

Critic Tom Shales

BARBARA BUSH

Your success as a family, our success as a society, depends not on what happens at the White House, but on what happens inside your house.

Barbara Bush

It's very hard to dislike someone who likes you. If someone thinks you're nice, you're apt to think their brilliant, have good judgment.

Barbara Bush

As you get older, I think you need to put your arms around each other more.

Barbara Bush on her secret for staying happily married

Joy

Barbara Bush, on what she meant when she said that former New York mayor Ed Koch was full of it

DONALD AND IVANA TRUMP, ETC.

Marla Maples: Are you in love with your husband? Because I am.

Ivana Trump: Stay away from my husband.

Maples: I love him, and if you don't, why don't you let him go?

Ivana: You stay away from my husband, or else.

Donald: You're overreacting.

> *Dialogue [pieced together by* TIME] *between Marla Maples and Ivana Trump upon their first face-to-face meeting*

Trump Ups The Ante To $100,000,000

> *NEW YORK NEWSDAY*

Trump: The War

> *NEW YORK DAILY NEWS*

Marla Boasts To Her Pals About Donald: Best Sex I Ever Had

> *NEW YORK POST*

I'm disgusted with my role in this. I've had to do 1,000 interviews, go on all these shows, pontificate, and I'm sick of myself. I could've said no, but it wouldn't have been fair to the paper, and in a way, my own aspirations and goals, even though I don't know what they are, really.

> *Gossip columnist Liz Smith, who broke the Donald and Ivana Trump breakup story*

Oh, flitter! Marla Maples did not break up Donald Trump's marriage. Ivana did.

> *Julia Rodgers*

It's bigger than Elizabeth Taylor and Richard Burton.

> *Donald Trump's evaluation of his divorce proceedings*

Marla is not money oriented. She is the type of girl who will get up in the morning and bake a cake for the doorman.

She even makes her own jams and jellies. At Christmas time she makes baskets and sweaters for people. That's where Marla comes from.

Marla Maples' former beau Tom Fitzgibbons

The reason they're giving for the divorce is that Donald has been having a long-term affair with himself.

Arsenio Hall on the Trump break-up

It appears that Marla Maples knows The Art of a Deal better than The Donald.

A. H. Cusack

He is very down to earth in his demands, and in his lifestyle, he's quite simple.

Ivana Trump, on her husband, December 1989

When the Trumps came, they put plastic Trump Castle ice buckets in each of the guest bedrooms. Well, you *just* don't do those things. . .

A maid at Mar-a-Lago, the Trump estate in Palm Beach

Trump Tower, Trump Plaza, Trump Parc, Trump Palace, Trump Castle, Trump Princess, Trump Shuttle, Trump Taj Mahal Casino.

The projects and properties named after Donald Trump by Donald Trump to date

I fight hard for victory, and I think I enjoy it as much as I ever did. But I realize that maybe new victories won't be the same as the first couple.

Donald Trump

Donald has never had the net worth he claimed. What he did have was trophy properties, brass balls, and a big mouth.

A lawyer and friend of Donald Trump

Why is Donald Trump such a good tennis player?
Because he swings both ways.
Why does Trump's wife have a gold diaphragm?
Because Donald likes to come into money.
What is the definition of skyjacking?
Masturbating in the Trump Shuttle

Joe Mastrianni

UH-OWE

NEW YORK POST headline

TRUMP IN A SLUMP

NEW YORK DAILY NEWS headline

The 1990s sure aren't like the 1980s.

Donald Trump

TRANSITIONS

I want to be alone.

Famous line by Greta Garbo, from GRAND HOTEL. Quoted often as summing up her life. She died this year

For a person of such diminutive stature, Sammy Davis Jr. truly was larger than life.

Scott Breuninger on the passing of Sammy Davis Jr.

Every Black entertainer who came after [Sammy] Davis was spared some of the blows he had to take, because he took them first.

Journalist Paul Gray

He will be missed. To rephrase the last song in MY FAIR LADY, we have grown accustomed to Rex Harrison's face.

Gerald Peary on the death of Rex Harrison

I believe in taking a positive attitude toward the world. My hope still is to leave the world a little bit better than when I got here.

Cheryl Henson quoting her father, Muppets creator
Jim Henson, in her eulogy

Kermit . . . Miss Piggy . . . and the other mirthful mugs . . . are suddenly orphans.

Michelle O'Michel Roudevitch

Mr. Henson was a shining star in the often too violent world of children's entertainment.

Danielle Horvath

Ava Gardner probably represented more tempestuous passion and sex appeal than one marriage could ever contain.

Author Kitty Kelley on Ava Gardner (1986),
who died this year

She was the loveliest lady I had ever seen.

First husband, Mickey Rooney

She was a goddess. I would stare at her, literally stare, in wonder.

Second husband, bandleader Artie Shaw

I had to give up—she was too dangerous for me.

World-class playboy Claude Terrail, about his
affair with Ava Gardner

Honey, there comes a time when you've got to face the fact that you're an old broad. I've had a hell of a good time, so my face looks, well, lived-in. You won't find me standing in front of a mirror, weeping.

Ava Gardner on aging

WARREN BEATTY

The public does not want Warren Beatty to look like Dick Tracy. The public wants Dick Tracy to look like Warren Beatty.

Actor Paul Sorvino

How come when you wear this jacket you look like Dick Tracy but when I wear it I look like a pimp?

Arsenio Hall to Warren Beatty

In a way, I'd rather ride down the street on a camel than give what is sometimes called an in-depth interview. I'd rather ride down the street on a camel nude. In a snowstorm. Backwards.

Warren Beatty talking about his attitude toward the press

ROSEANNE BARR

[Roseanne Barr]'s such a blockhead. She gets a splinter in her finger every time she scratches her forehead.

International Dull Folks Unlimited

He showed honeymoon pictures of us from the *National Enquirer* in bathing suits. It's not a pretty sight, and we know that.

*Tom Arnold, Roseanne Barr's husband on why
he's mad at Arsenio Hall*

The closest sound to Rosanne Barr's singing the National Anthem was my cat being neutered.

Johnny Carson

RICHARD NIXON

What happened in Watergate—the facts, not the myths—was wrong. In retrospect, while I was not involved in the decision to conduct the break-in, I should have set a higher standard for the conduct of the people who participated in my campaign and administration. I should have established a moral tone that would have made such actions unthinkable. I did not. I played by the rules of politics as I found them. Not taking a higher road than my predecessors and my adversaries was my central mistake.

Former President Richard Nixon in his book, IN THE ARENA

No one can recover spiritually from a major loss without the help of others.

Richard Nixon

Anyone who thinks Japan is going to export democracy to China must be smoking pot.

Richard Nixon

Nixon didn't just defeat his opponents. He destroyed them, personally as well as politically. Richard Nixon changed the map of American Presidential electoral politics.

Roger Morris in RICHARD M. NIXON: THE RISE OF AN
AMERICAN POLITICIAN

The thing that's endlessly intriguing about Nixon is that he dominates and personifies American politics for three decades, both its best and its worst parts. His own progression mirrors the country's, from a virulent anti-Communist to being the author of detente to now being an observer of Gorbachev's reforms.

Journalist John F. Stacks

RYAN WHITE

He was a special child thrown into special circumstances and he just rode on that circumstance.

*The doctor of Ryan White, the Indiana teenager
who died from AIDS*

Although his courageous battle has reached its end, Ryan is now safe in the arms of God. He and his family stand as a symbol of the need for greater tolerance and understanding toward those afflicted with AIDS.

Ronald Reagan

After seeing a person like Ryan White—as a fine and loving and gentle person—it was hard for people to justify discrimination against people who suffer from this terrible disease.

Thomas Brandt of the National Commission on AIDS

Ryan's death reaffirms that we as a people must pledge to continue the fight, his fight against this dreaded disease.

President George Bush

MARION BARRY

My mind's too sharp, my body too precious, to foul it with drugs.

What D.C. Mayor Marion Barry used to preach to high school students

Goddam, I shouldn't have come up here . . . that bitch set me up.

Marion Barry as shown in the videotape played at his trial for drug possession

I would let him in the house. I would give him a bag and he gave me money. He would give me $200. . . .

Lydia Pearson, testifying that she sold crack cocaine to D.C. Mayor Marion Barry "about 25 times"

I'm back and I feel good about the treatment program. I feel good about myself.

Marion Barry

Many of my supporters and political polls have indicated that if I were to run, I could win. . . . What good does it do to win the battle if in the process I lose my soul?

Marion Barry

This certainly is a terrible situation and it's certainly the worst thing I've been through in my life.

Christopher, the ten-year-old son of Marion Barry

AND SO FORTH

The grass is not, in fact, always greener on the other side of the fence. Fences have nothing to do with it. The grass is greenest where it is watered.

Robert Fulgham

If we're all guilty of projection, what does it mean when we say "I love you"?

David D. Kim

You can see how serious it is, so please keep the faith in God, keep the faith in me and please say a prayer for me.

Teen-age actor Corey Feldman giving an anti-drug warning to fans after his arrest on cocaine and heroin charges

I'm not perfect, but those flaws make up an interesting person.

Mary Frann, actress

The most important part in any car is a sober driver.

From a slogan in a Mothers Against Drunk Driving advertisement

. . . There are men who are flirtatious and womanizing—but if someone is looking for romance, this is a person you don't look to.

Goldie Hawn, on her BIRD ON A WIRE co-star Mel Gibson

If you act like a loose cannon, people tend to treat you with kid gloves.

Mark Heller

I stand fearlessly for small dogs, the American flag, motherhood and the Bible. That's why people love me.

Art Linkletter, best known for his TV show,
"People Are Funny"

He's the greatest husband in the world and he's nothing to brag about.

Marlo Thomas, on husband Phil Donahue

I have to say that the thing I enjoyed most, because it was so preposterous, was the issue of *People* that named me one of the world's 50 most beautiful people. I think I followed Michelle Pfeiffer.

Jane Pauley, on her seemingly unending canonization
by the media

You know, I look like a duck. I just do. And I'm not the only person who thinks that. It's the way my mouth sort of curls up, or my nose tilts up. I should have played Howard the Duck.

Actress Michelle Pfeiffer

Actress Kim Basinger
Actress Julia Roberts
Model Claudia Schiffer
Actress Isabel Adjani
Actress Sherilyn Fenn
Actress Cybill Shepherd
Actress Nicollette Sheridan
Singer Janet Jackson
Actress Michelle Pfeiffer
Model Cindy Crawford

The world's ten most beautiful women according to
US magazine

Any list of the world's most beautiful women that doesn't mention my wife Kim isn't worth the paper it's printed on.

Hank Graham

Yeah, I read history. But it doesn't make you nice. Hitler read history, too.

Joan Rivers

I drank after the theater and I found I was allergic to alcohol—I broke out in drunks. I knew I had to go out and get some help, and I am a recovering alcoholic today.

Actor Robert Morse

Just because I'm a woman who speaks my mind about things and doesn't behave like some stupid blonde bimbo doesn't mean that I'm aggressive.

Irish pop star Sinead O'Connor

He who laughs, lasts.

Author Robert Fulgham

What he showed me was not what I had to get, but what I already have. I am just myself, and who I am is a lot.

"Cosby" star Phylicia Rashad explaining her devotion to the late Swami Muktananda

With all of my heart and soul, I want all of you to understand that what you call the world out there is rough. It's rough not only in terms of your job but in terms of your personal relationships. You'll have many, many friends, but if your relationship with your mate is 100 percent of your heart, you'll never need a friend.

Bill Cosby, giving a commencement address at the University of Notre Dame

Barbara [Walters] never viewed sex as a priority, and it didn't exist in our relationship. It was apparent that it was not important to her.

Alexis Lichine

I should have started eight years ago, instead of this year, where there just hasn't been enough time to get to meet enough of the wonderful people in Georgia.

Andrew Young explaining his loss in the governor's race in Georgia

At 82, I feel like a 20-year-old but, unfortunately, there's never one around.

Milton Berle

From the hips up, I'm OK. Until you get to the top of my head, where I have to wear toupees. But then, I've been wearing toupees since the '20s.

George Burns, who turned 94 last year, evaluating his physical condition

You'd be surprised how many people would have done what I did.

Jerry Schemmel, who ran back into a crashed DC-10 to rescue a child

Life is like a B-grade movie. You don't want to leave in the middle of it, but you don't want to see it again.

Ted Turner

When you come down to it, I guess I'm a firm believer in the idea that if there's any way you can postpone reality— you should.

Chloe Webb

If there's no possibility of failure, there's no challenge.

Mountain climber Adrian Crane

Steve McQueen was the best . . . Burt Reynolds was the worst.

Mamie Van Doren, on the men she slept with

Life is too short to worry about the wrinkles in your jeans.

Donnie Wahlberg, New Kids on the Block singer

I'd like to be in public office. Hey, I'll never lie, I'll always tell you the truth, and I'll work really hard, which is more than I can say for almost every public official that I know.

Cher

I have no personal life at the moment and that's liberating.

Carol Burnett

I don't think Dan Aykroyd would be as funny if he were built like a marathon runner. I find it refreshing that people like Dan let their bodies go to seed.

Liam Neeson

Maybe the lesson of history is that there are no lessons from history.

George Stern

In the 1990s, the public is going to realize that their taxpayer dollars are going to their [corporate] enemies.

Ralph Nader

I now need to take a very aggressive approach to having a baby.

News anchorwoman Connie Chung on her hopes of becoming a mother

The sexual act is one of the most primitive methods of mooring oneself at least temporarily to something or someone.

Rosemary Stoyle

Beauty comes from within. It is sparked by an inner strength and radiance that goes far beyond physical appearance.

Janet Jackson

My trick for looking and feeling young is being constantly on the go, meeting new people, seeing new things.

Diane Von Furstenberg

The great revolutionary of the early 20th Century was not Lenin, who ignored the force of nationalism and insisted on his narrow-minded dogma of class struggle. It was no less narrow-minded Woodrow Wilson, with his insistence on the—potentially disastrous—principle of self-determination.

Historian John Lukas

Real equality is going to come not when a female Einstein is recognized as quickly as a male Einstein, but when a female schlemiel is promoted as quickly as a male schlemiel.

Bella Abzug, as quoted by Marlo Thomas

Once you give up integrity, the rest is a piece of cake.

Author Paul Slansky quoting a line of J.R. from "Dallas"

I have a lifetime appointment and I intend to serve it. I expect to die at 110, shot by a jealous husband.

Supreme Court Justice Thurgood Marshall

Rare is the person who can weigh the faults of others without putting his thumb on the scales.

Byron J. Langenfield

Trust your hunches. They're usually based on facts filed away just below the conscious level.

Dr. Joyce Brothers

Having it all doesn't necessarily mean having it all at once.

Stephanine Luetkehans

No one can make you feel inferior without your consent.

Steven Harris quoting Eleanor Roosevelt

You must not only drive cars, but build them; not only ride planes, but design and fly them.

Jesse Jackson to young Black Americans

Tina Turner and Eddie Murphy

The most exciting Black woman and Black man according to the readers of EBONY

Actor Alec Baldwin
Actor Gregg Rainwater
Actor Kiefer Sutherland
John F. Kennedy, Jr.
Actor Keanu Reeves
Actor John Stamos
Actor Tom Cruise
Actor Matt Dillon

The sexiest bachelors according to US *magazine*

Money is like a sixth sense, without which you cannot make use of the other five.

W. Somerset Maugham as quoted in an advertisement for WORKING ASSETS MONEY FUND

Self-esteem is a good thing, but anyone who has ever toilet trained a child knows that it is possible to make rather too much of the efforts of the child on the potty; one wonders if little Ed was told once too often what a great thing he'd done and began to think that all that emanated from his being was pretty great.

Peggy Noonan reviewing ALL THE BEST *by former New York mayor Ed Koch*

She used to tell her friends that every woman needs at least three men: one for sex, one for money, and one for fun.

Shana Alexander, on Bess Myerson

Economic news is bad because *most* news is bad. We concentrate on the one house that burns down rather than the 1000 that have just been built.

"Adam Smith"

If you lower your standards you deserve everything you get.

Thomas Melohn

Every time you get knocked down you get up stronger.
Marlon Brando's personal philosophy

If you had only six months to live, what would you do,
and if you're not doing that now, why not?
Stephen Thomas

I'm a fellow who works in the vineyard of compromise.
Congressman Dan Rostenkowski

Are you kidding? For me to make lasagna would be a desecration of a great Italian dish. I let my mother make lasagna. I let my mother-in-law make lasagna. I let [my wife]
Matilda make lasagna. I don't mess with sacred things.
New York governor Mario Cuomo

[James] Woods couldn't have a consistent relationship with
a doorknob.
Actress Sean Young

There's no deodorant like success.
Elizabeth Taylor

The difference between a mountain and a molehill is your
perspective.
Al Neuharth

I always try to balance the light with the heavy—a few
tears for the human spirit in with the sequins and the
fringes.
Bette Midler

The best way to prepare for the future is to take care of
the present.
Columnist Robert J. Samuelson

Now that I'm pregnant I feel beautiful for the first time in
my life.
Fashion model Karen Alexander

I am divorced and support myself, and I often call on three wonderful supportive males. I'm proud to say that my two sons and my father always come through. This doesn't make me less of a woman, either in my eyes or in theirs.

Denise K. Rose

We drive through life with our brakes on, and one of those brakes is low self-esteem.

James Newman, the Los Angeles County
Self-Esteem Task Force Chairman

Anyone who can marry that many times, gain and lose that much weight, refer to Montgomery Clift as a friend, star in WHO'S AFRAID OF VIRGINIA WOOLF? and X, Y AND ZEE is not only extremely bearable but has something to teach.

Playwright Wendy Wasserstein, on Elizabeth Taylor

It's my most successful late-night production.

Former late-night talk show host Pat Sajak,
on the pregnancy of his wife

The only real risk is the risk of thinking too small.

Social commentator Frances Moore Lappe

The epidemic of drug and violence in the black community stems from a calculated attempt by whites to force black self-destruction.

Louis Farrakhan

If I would believe what I read about myself, I would hate my guts, too.

Zsa Zsa Gabor

It is true that when I was 14 years old I became pregnant. The baby was born prematurely and died shortly after birth. The experience was the most emotional, confusing and traumatic of my young life.

Talk show hostess Oprah Winfrey

I've had enough pretending. I'm officially moving in with my friend, Martin Rabbat. We have been lovers for 12 years now and are building a house on the beach [in Hawaii] which will be our home. And too bad for people who are upset by it.

Actor Richard Chamberlain as quoted in an interview with
NOUS DEUX, a French women's magazine.

Often it is cheaper to buy something than to accept it as a gift.

Richard C. Miller

I'm more interested in becoming the greatest mother that ever lived than the greatest movie star.

Actress Amy Irving

I take a lot of crap, a lot of insults, a lot of humiliation. Some of it's self-generated and some of it is promulgated by people who see only this neolithic, primordial image. I'm not a right-wing jingoistic human being. Rambo is. He's psychotic. In many ways.

Actor Sylvester Stallone

I think I exploded the myth that rock and roll is just for young people.

47-year-old singer Paul McCartney
on a sold-out Los Angeles concert

There is nothing more irrelevant than a former politician.

Congressman Jim Leach

My act was senseless, yours is a choice based on fairness and the law. I know I am asking for a chance I did not give those boys [I shot in 1978].

Plea by death row inmate Robert Alton Harris to California
Governor George Deukmejian

Death will be a great relief. No more interviews.

Katharine Hepburn

I was in the third grade, and my oldest sister was in the sixth or seventh grade. Her girlfriends were starting to go out with boys and would practice on me—put me on top of the sink and teach me how long to kiss. For hours.

Actor Tom Cruise

Unfortunately, politicians have the Paul Masson theory of government—"we will deal with no problem before its time."

Mervin Field, California pollster

If all else fails, read the directions.

Walter Green

Real people grow up and go on to other things. But real people feel that celebrities should always stay the same. That's what happened to me.

Singer Donny Osmond, on the comeback trail

The drug war will be won or lost based on our education and treatment programs not on how many people we arrest.

Robert Stutman, ex-Chief of Drug Enforcement Administration's New York City office

I touch the future, I teach.

Cynthia Ann Broad, quoting Christa McAuliff

It's totally okay to be a normie.

Former alcoholic and drug abuser 15-year-old actress Drew Barrymore

Apartheid must go, and it must go now. The masses of the American people are with us. Both Congress and the Senate of the United States are with us. President Bush and the administration are with us. Surely apartheid will go.

Nelson Mandela

I love you, Daddy, come home, please come home. I love you, Daddy. Come home. Send me to the circus.

Sulome Anderson, daughter of hostage Terry Anderson on the fifth anniversary of his captivity

Gonna miss you bunches.

Deborah Norville saying goodbye to Jane Pauley on "The Today Show"

You are slowly changing into a Caesar.

Editor Adam Michnik to Solidarity Leader Lech Walesa

We can now mothball the word "superpower." The Soviet Union, which use to be one, is unraveling, and the United States, which still talks like one, is becoming irrelevant.

Columnist Russell Baker

I've never owned a fur, and I don't smoke. But I've had it with these granola heads trying to palm their emotional guilt trip off on the rest of society. If they don't want to smoke cigarettes, swat flies, boil lima beans or put chickens through the emotional torment of parent-egg separation, fine. Let them get their own town, go off and feel bad together.

Julie Neuffer

He demolished people. . . . You either loved him or you hated him, but there was no one remotely like him, except, maybe, Lucifer.

Doris Lilly on old flame, director John Huston

The only reason I would take up jogging would be so I could hear heavy breathing again.

Erma Bombeck

Ahhhh, the man is tragically gorgeous. . . . He starts like a bull, stamping the ground with his foot, and comes at me with a raging something and jumps on me, and we break the bed. . . . He is very agile, I can't believe he's 64.

Actress Lolita Davidovich commenting on co-star
Paul Newman

If my eyes should ever turn brown, my career is shot to hell.

Actor Paul Newman

There are no mistakes, only lessons.

NEW AGE JOURNAL

Lessons are repeated until they are learned.

NEW AGE JOURNAL

I was sobbing and late to work, and you know I would go out to my car at the end of the night and just sit in the car and cry.

Soap actress Genie Francis, on the pressure that led her to
leave "General Hospital"

I can't talk to beautiful women—there's always that fear of rejection. In high school, I was a geek—I still haven't recovered.

"China Beach" co-star Brian Wimmer

If we don't get an answer, we will, strengthened by the support we receive, try to overthrow the government.

Actress turned animal rights crusader Brigitte Bardot

Don't come [to Washington, D.C]. The values are warped. If I could find a way to make a living, I would be back in the heartland in a minute.

Former Reagan Domestic Policy Adviser Gary Bauer

I think for a woman just to use her looks and to be an actress or a model is sad—a woman should use her brain.

Author Jackie Collins

Even when opportunity knocks, a person has to get off his
rear end and answer the door.

Ann Landers

Congress and the State shall have the authority to enact
laws, making lying by a politician a crime, punishable by
public paddling on their bare bottoms.

Columnist Mike Royko

I would like to meet Mikhail Gorbachev. I think it would
be great to sit in a room with him . . . and try to make
peace.

Singer Donnie Wahlberg of New Kids on the Block

Even when I know it isn't true, some little part of me always
clings to the hope that everything would be different if I
just had a new color of lipstick.

From "Cathy" by Cathy Guisewite

I never said I'd solve all the problems.

Former New York mayor Ed Koch

If you don't get tough on drugs, they will get tough on
you.

Drug czar William Bennett

The price we pay for freedom of expression is that some
things will be considered vile by some people. . . But what's
vile to a Mormon family in Utah is not vile to a black family
in south central Los Angeles.

Danny Goldberg

If you pet me, I'll purr. But if you hit me, I might scratch,
of course.

Billionaire Leona Helmsley

I thought I was getting to first base but it turned out to be
square one.

Cartoonist Thaves, in the comic strip "Frank and Ernest"

Tact is the art of making guests feel at home when you wish they really were.

Sarah Kinghan

We all love animals, but why do we call some of them pets and some of them dinner?

Grammy winning singer k.d. lang in a public service spot for the People for the Ethical Treatment of Animals

You can't have everything. Where would you put it?

Ann Landers

Why is it that every man I meet used up all his "nice" years on someone else, and only finds me when he is cranky and inflexible?

"Cathy" by cartoonist Cathy Guisewite

If after 17 years of marriage you're single again, I don't care how many awards you have and how much money, it's terrifying.

Jane Fonda

I think the transition from boy to man has taken me, probably, about two and a half years. I am actually a man now, whereas six months ago . . . I was probably still verging on boy.

Fine Young Cannibals singer Roland Gift

I want [the young people of Virginia] to know that oppression can be lifted, that discrimination can be eliminated, that poverty need not be binding, that disability can be overcome, and that the offer of opportunity in a free society carries with it the requirement of hard work, the rejection of drugs and other false highs, and the willingness to work with others whatever their color or national origin.

L. Douglas Wilder, the nation's first black governor of Virginia in his inaugural address

I will not eat oysters. I want my food dead. Not sick, not wounded, dead.

Woody Allen

I've never been afraid of death, but I know he is waiting at the corner. . . . I've been trained to kill and to save, so has everyone else. I am frightened of what lays beyond the fog, and yet . . . do not mourn for me. Revel in the life that I have died to give you . . . but most of all, don't forget the Army was my choice. Something that I wanted to do. Remember I joined the Army to serve my country and ensure that you are free to do what you want and live your lives freely.

Taken from a letter to his mother by Private First Class James Markwell, a 20-year-old Army medic who was one of the first killed in the Panama invasion. Quoted by President Bush in the State of the Union message.

I certainly don't want a woman giving up a good job and following me to take care of me—that's no life for her or me.

Actor Joe Penny

President Reagan was not able to get this story correct in retrospect . . . it is not surprising that he did not understand it when it was going on.

David Broder on the Reagan testimony for the Poindexter trial

We mark today not a victory of party or the accomplishments of an individual but the triumph of an idea, an idea as old as America, as old as the God who looks out for us all . . . the idea that all men and women are created equal . . .

L. Douglas Wilder, first black governor in the United States

Nine years ago, I was selling [my] blood in Los Angeles for $12.00 a pint, $14.00 if I could pull somebody in with me on the buddy system, literally to buy booze, so I could drink that day.

Actor John Larroquette, commenting on his former alcoholism

I'd like to dispel the myth that when you put a wedding ring on a woman, her brain stops.

Marilyn Quayle

In order to keep a true perspective of one's importance, everyone should have a dog that will worship him and a cat that will ignore him.

Dereke Bruce

Even though she's on in years, she has an enormously powerful impact on the children's lives. She is as much if not more of a presence than she was when she was more active. She still has an indescribable force and time has not diminished it.

Senator Ted Kennedy on his mother
Rose Kennedy's 100 birthday

Did you know that Jesse Helms was a regular contributor to a white supremacist magazine?

From a 900 DUMP HELMS phone line

Someone told me I should run for the Senate because I'm also a wizard under the sheets.

Former Louisiana governor Edwin Edwards, on former
Klansman David Duke's plans to run for the Senate

The case she presents is ridiculous. She was a friend whom I tried to help. Someone obviously got to her and convinced her that she could possibly make a killing by suing me.

William Shatner commenting on a palimony suit filed by one
time friend, Vera Montes, against him

I don't think I have ever talked to a teenager (who was) more excited. He yelled on the phone, "I really did it!" and it actually was a yell.

Martha Wilkinson, quoting country singer Waylon Jennings
reporting on having passed the G.E.D.

I'm not dead—I just appear that way.

> *Red Skelton on hearing that in a survey 41%*
> *of the population thought he was dead*

The more you understand yourself, the better you can appreciate others.

> *P. M. H. Atwater*

Why do cabbies honk at non-cab drivers for driving the way cabbies do?

> *Columnist Herb Caen*

Let's leave some blue up above us, let's leave some green on the ground. It is only ours to borrow. Let's leave some for tomorrow. Leave it and pass it on down.

> *From a song by country music group Alabama*

In suicide, as in no other cause of death, the true victims are the ones who must live on after a loved one commits this selfish act.

> *Colleen Mastroianni*

I know as a candidate I should kiss your ass, but I haven't learned to do that with equanimity yet.

> *Boston University President and candidate*
> *for Governor of Massachusetts John Silber*

I'm more of a victim of democracy than I was of Bobby Lee Smith. At least he didn't do this to me for months. He didn't do it to me and then two months later come back and do it again.

> *Nancy Ziegenmeyer, a rape survivor, on delays in her trial*

The psychological violence at the hands of the defense attorney and judge was much worse than the violence of the street.

> *Model Marla Hanson whose face was slashed*
> *in a razor attack*

I am prouder of my registered nurse title than I am of my Miss America title. But Miss America is a title that gets me through a lot of doors.

Kay Lani Rae Rafko, Miss America 1988

There is so much more to me than my blackness, the color of my skin. . . .to tell the truth, Miss Mississippi had a tan that was darker than me.

Carole Jist, the first black Miss U.S.A.

Success is the best revenge.

Deposed (1983) Miss America Vanessa Williams

I was Miss Congeniality in the Miss Teenage America Pageant. I don't tell that to many people — I've always felt that was so embarrassing. But really — that's really who I am. That's me.

Actress Cybill Shepherd

Flattery is like chewing gum. Enjoy it but don't swallow it.

Mrs. Wilson in "Dennis the Menace" by Hank Ketcham

Morton Downey Jr. with a Ph.D.

Nickname for White House Chief of Staff John Sununu

I lost a velvet cowl scarf of Donna's [Karan] today on a plane. I don't think I can live without it.

TV personality Kathleen Sullivan

For too long, and unfairly to boot, he was the Rodney Dangerfield of former presidents. But Jimmy Carter has been redeeming himself with good works, capping a stellar comeback with a truly magnificent performance in Nicaragua's low-flash point election.

Editorial in THE PHILADELPHIA INQUIRER

What a catch. Great face. Great body. Great mother-in-law.

Talent agent Peg Donegan of John F. Kennedy Jr.

I neither was nor am a holier-than-thou. I've seen about everything, heard just about everything and done part of it.

Senator Jesse Helms

We're definitely going to be together, and we need to figure out details. He lives in Boston, but that would be difficult for me because I have three children and their fathers now live in Los Angeles.

Cybill Shepherd on her new bicoastal relationship

Does this mean I'm not on the CIA payroll anymore?

Manuel Noriega, according to cartoonist Toles

When Rosa Parks went public with her pain and refused to ride in the back of the bus, she released energy, the energy to take a giant step in righting a great wrong and to lift many a burden.

Browne Barr

[Imelda Marcos used the New York branch of the Philippine National Bank as] her own personal piggy bank. She cracked it open and had bundles of cash delivered to her so that she could buy art works and jewels.

Assistant U.S. Attorney Debra Livingston at the racketeering trial of Imelda Marcos

I might be an antique like the Stones, but antiques are valuable.

Billy Joel

I need substance in my life. And the world needs substance. The world doesn't need anymore hip. Hip is dead. The world doesn't need more cool. . . . We need more Picassos, more Mozarts, more John Singer Sargents, not more Milli Vanillis. Not more haircuts.

Billy Joel

As far as I'm concerned, there won't be a Beatles reunion as long as John Lennon remains dead.

Former Beatle George Harrison

We never said, "Let's go out and be lesbians." It was really like this: let's just be girlfriends—silly, juvenile girlfriends. The whole lesbian thing being read into it was just stupid, ridiculous.

Comedian Sandra Bernhard on her relationship with rock singer Madonna

In the old days, if you "did it," you couldn't talk about it. Now if you don't do it, you can't tell anybody.

Susan Rodstein

To say that Secord worked under my direction would say a Major General is working for a Lieutenant Colonel and I don't think that's accurate.

Oliver North testifying at the Iran-Contra trial of John Poindexter before he admitted he did give direction to Major General Richard Secord in the Contra supply operation

Excuse the mess but we live here.

Roseanne Barr

Assume nothing. Inside every dumb blond there may be a very smart brunette.

Ann Landers

I don't want to spend taxpayers' money in a court proceeding.

Marilyn Louise Harrell, "Robin HUD," explaining why she decided to plead guilty to the charges against her of defrauding millions of tax dollars

I must use the manure that has been thrown on me to fertilize myself and grow from seed again.

Eartha Kitt

Sincerity is everything. If you can fake that, you've got it made.

Comedian George Burns

Small minds ask small questions.

White House Chief of Staff John Sununu

I'd rather not be introduced as a former White House aide or a former lieutenant colonel, both of which I was, but as a husband of one and father of four. I got that backward one time on the campaign trail a while ago. Funny thing was, I was in San Francisco and nobody noticed.

Oliver North

Constraints are not necessarilynegative. They may force you to try avenues you would have ignored.

Architect Cesar Pelli

I wouldn't trade places with anybody. I'm growing up. I'm really growing up. And I think that I'm getting better because of it.

Oprah Winfrey

And Michael Dukakis, oh boy. Popularity really plummeting there. In fact, even Willie Horton is claiming, "Look, I hardly even knew the guy."

Jay Leno

Again, you change as you get older.

Sinead O'Connor commenting on the fact that she let some hair grow on her head

Some people see me as nutty, but I'm still committed to my beliefs—more than ever. I'm quite serious, but I guess people laugh because I'm not a professor. I'm someone out there using this in my own life. They wouldn't laugh at the Dalai Lama.

Actress Shirley MacLaine

The archetypes of women are the madonna and the whore. We're all like that, but we repress one side or the other.

Actress Laura Dern

To be anthropocentric is to remain unaware of the limits of human nature.

Entomologist Edward O. Wilson

Sometimes in the heat of political battle people lose site of the ultimate objective and tactics become ends in themselves. That's a mistake.

Senator George Mitchell

A continental nation blessed with liberty, natural resources and diverse people. . . a nation that saved Europe twice from itself, put a man on the moon, shed an institution and legacy of racial shame, and created a culture imitated around the globe—such a nation cannot accept some miniature ambition.

Senator Bill Bradley

Tears and weeping are mere self-indulgence if, in the final analysis, we don't act to find and implement alternatives to hatred, injustice and violence in all forms.

Nobel Peace Prize recipient Mairead Corrigan Maguire

Hatred is entrenched in human nature. . . . It slumbers in all of us. It can awaken an any time. I am not sure if we can eradicate hate from our hearts, but of this I am certain: it must always be our goal.

Soviet writer Anatoly Rybakov

When I came out of Wounded Knee, I was not even healed up [from the birth of my first baby], but they put me in jail at Pine Ridge and took my baby away. I could not nurse. My breasts swelled up and grew hard as rocks, hurting badly. In 1975 the feds put the muzzles of their M-16s against my head, threatening to blow me away. It's hard being an Indian woman.

Mary Crow Dog in LAKOTA WOMAN

The great surprise of human evolution may be that the highest form of selfishness is selflessness.

Robert Ornstein and David Sobel

What democracy needs is public debate, not information.

Christopher Lasch

I left high school a virgin.

Actor Tom Selleck

Bores bore each other, too, but it never seems to teach them anything.

Tom Marquis

I am not saying he did not do it, I simply had my doubts.

Juror Richard Silensky, on the not guilty verdict in the case against John Gotti, reputed boss of the nation's most powerful crime family

Most admired female black Americans:
  Oprah Winfrey, Coretta Scott King, Maya Angelou
Most admired male black Americans:
  Bill Cosby, Jesse Jackson

According to readers of EBONY

America's dullest celebrities:
  Roseanne Barr
  Danny DeVito
  Arsenio Hall
  Dan Quayle
  Connie Chung

According to International Dull Folks Unlimited

And what all is more normal than failure? What more in common than to rise greatly above failure or disadvantage?

James D. Griffin, QUOTE MAGAZINE

Shame on [*People Magazine*] for choosing Sean Connery as the Sexiest Man Alive. Mr. Connery has admitted that he approves of slapping women. . . . I nominate Sean Connery as the "Sexist Man Alive."

Laurie Gilbert

Chapter 2

THE NATION

POLITICS

It is we who drive the politician to use jargon, words that evade and obscure the truth. It is we who make them say that troops are "advisors," that war plans are "scenarios" that invasions are "incursions."

The late Henry Fairlie

I have often thought that if there had been a good rap group around in those days I might have chosen a career in music instead of politics.

Richard Nixon, looking wistfully back on his early days and his love of music at the conclusion of a lengthy interview in THE NEW YORK TIMES

If foreign policy is conducted by those who consider the moral dimension an irritant, if not an obstacle, we should not be surprised by the victory of our enemy.

Christopher Manion

Perhaps the most frustrating consequence of the Reagan presidency was that it forced the nation to refight the civil rights battles that had been won during the 1960s and 1970s.

Ralph G. Ness

For forty years [the CIA] usually overestimated both the size of the Soviet economy and its rate of growth. This in turn has persistently distorted our estimates of the Soviet threat, notably in the 1980s when we turned ourselves into a debtor nation to pay for the arms to counter the threat of a nation whose home front, unbeknown to us, was collapsing.

Senator Daniel Patrick Moynihan

[Watergate] was neither trivial nor insignificant. It raised important, painful questions about American political behavior in the American political system, questions that speak to the traditions and structure of American life. Whether the actors and the drama of Watergate confronted those questions successfully or unsuccessfully, directly or passively, honestly or conveniently, will be the subject of history. That is the significant, inescapable importance of Watergate.

Stanley I. Cutler in THE WARS OF WATERGATE:
THE LAST CRISIS OF RICHARD NIXON

All the isms are wasms—except one, the most powerful ism of this century, indeed, of the entire democratic age, which is nationalism.

Historian John Lucas

We've indicted more public officials in the last eighteen months than were indicted in the last ten years.

Dexter Lehtinen, acting U.S. Attorney in Miami

Prematurely terminated flight: Crash.

Prime example of military double speak collected by Canadian and United States Organization of English Teachers

The federal agency created to handle the sale of insolvent thrifts has set an annual budget for legal fees of $130 million. That's quadruple the cumulative $33 million it has spent on lawyers since its inception last year.

TIME

Marxist-Leninists used to talk about their "permanent revolution," but as it turns out the only permanent revolution the world has ever seen is the American Revolution.

Jack Kemp, Secretary of Housing and Urban Development

The State of the Union depends on whether we help our neighbor, claim the problems of our community as our own. We've got to step forward when there is trouble, lend a hand, be what I call a point of light to a stranger in need.

President George Bush in the State of the Union message

The 1990s should be "The Decade for America." We have done a good job defending the world. We have won. Communism is a failure. Now we have more resources for our children.

Congresswoman Barbara Boxer

New Hampshire (32.1%) and Louisiana (2.1%).

States with the highest and lowest, respectively, percentage of state legislators who are women

You'd have to be awfully spoiled if you lived the life we live and wished for something else.

Barbara Bush on life in the White House

And I know this about the American people: We welcome competition, we'll match our ingenuity, our energy, our experience and technology, our spirit and enterprise against anyone. But let the competition be free, but let is also be fair. America is ready.

President George Bush

War Is Our Profession—Peace Is Our Product.

New motto of the Strategic Air Command
(Old motto: "Peace Is Our Profession.")

A true test of one's commitment to constitutional principles is the extent to which recognition is given to the rights of those in our midst who are the least affluent, least powerful and least welcome.

New York federal district-court Judge Leonard Sand

And so, after berating Timothy Ryan, 44, for his utter un-preparedness for the job, the Senate last week approved his appointment to head the Office of Thrift Supervision by a generous 62-37 vote.

TIME

The teflon wears thin. One year after the presidency, citizens Ron and Nancy have become a couple whom everyone loves to hate.

Title on LOS ANGELES *magazine cover*

I'm not sure Jesse even knows where Southwest [Washington, D.C.] is. Right now the city needs a full-time mayor. Jesse would be good if you want a figurehead mayor, a cheerleader. I need more than that.

Lloyd Reeves

I am afraid when I need him I may look up and he's in the U.S.S.R. holding someone else's hand.

Lillian Wiggins, commenting on the possibility of Jesse Jackson becoming mayor of Washington, D.C.

Congress would have him where they want him and would make his life miserable. He would have to show measurable progress to be creditable but Congress would be skeptical about giving him victories. Congress wouldn't give him the money he would need.

Ronald Walters, commenting on the possibility of Jesse Jackson becoming mayor of Washington, D.C.

"The peace dividend"—that is money we would have spent on defense that would not be required if events keep moving in the direction that they are now moving.

Unknown

[People join private clubs because] they like to be with their friends, just like Hispanics like to be with their friends or blacks like to be with their friends.

Senator Alan Simpson

President Reagan cited a poor memory as the answer to over 120 questions about the Iran Contra case in videotaped testimony at the trial of John M. Poindexter.

According to network news

After identifying these problems, [President Bush] is content to nibble at the edges of them, rather than grapple with both hands, as our great presidents have done with the tests of their times.

David S. Broder commenting on President Bush's budget

If you're in the first or second year of a presidential cycle, absent external events the President is always going to get the lion's share of what he wants.

Representative David R. Obey

[The politicians are] in the business of brokering the tax revenue. What keeps them in office is not their talent for oratory but their skill at redistributing the national income in a way that rewards their constituents, clients, patrons, and friends. They trade in every known commodity—school lunches, tax exemptions, water and mineral rights, aluminum siding, dairy subsidies, pension subsidies, highway contracts, prison uniforms—and they work believers of government like gamblers pulling at slot machines.

Lewis H. Lapham

The Democratic leaders in the Congress . . . have formed something close to a coalition government with a Republican administration.

Investment banker Felix Rohatyn

Never kick a man when he is up.

Congressman Thomas S. Foley quoting former Congressman Tip O'Neill

GOVERNMENT SPENDING

Maybe the deficit will float away on hot air

> *Title of a* WASHINGTON POST *article on President Bush's*
> *new budget*

People don't feel any sense of ownership over the federal government . . . It isn't them, and it isn't theirs.

> *Democratic pollster Geoffrey Garin*

Ironically, the fiscal years that were not preceded by budget summits actually resulted in a most real deficit reduction.

> *According to a report by the Tax Foundation*

The results of prior budget summits have been higher taxes, higher spending, and higher deficits.

> *Economist Paul Craig Roberts*

One of the prices we pay for democracy is the money we have to put into defense.

> *Former New Jersey governor Thomas H. Kean*

The national debt is around $10,000 a person, or $40,000 for a family of four.

> *Columnist Michael Kinsley*

All individual federal-income-tax dollars collected in those states [west of the Mississippi] in 1989 will buy absolutely nothing. . . . Every dime . . . will be needed to pay interest on the national debt for one year.

> *Lee Iacocca*

The federal government spends only about $127 million annually to aid adult-literacy efforts. But about $5 billion in taxpayer dollars goes for public assistance each year to grown-ups who can't get jobs because of illiteracy.

> *Al Neuharth*

If you don't drink, smoke or drive a car, you're a tax evader.

Speaker of the House of Representatives Tom Foley

Eight years of Reaganomics saddled each U.S. adult with a $2762.00 bill.

According to Adrian W. Thorp, a former senior staff economist in the Reagan Administration

The tax law, in a large part, may no longer be administrable by the Internal Revenue Service, and no longer comprehensible by most taxpayers and their advisers.

Lawrence Gibbs, former IRS Commissioner, relaying the concerns of many tax authorities

You have to learn to read and write, son—you'll be filling out federal forms all your life!

From a cartoon by Baloo

It's getting to be a morning ritual in Washington. Gather around the budget table and pass the rhetoric.

NBC news commentator Faith Daniels

The best cure for the national economy would be economy.

Ashley Cooper

There can be no doubt that, sometime around 1995 or so, the current federal budget deficits will disappear.

Charles R. Morris in THE COMING GLOBAL BOOM

The American constitution was designed to make it hard to have too much government. But what we've had too little of is responsible government.

Senator Daniel Patrick Moynihan

I'd like to see any savings that we can get [from reducing defense spending used] to reduce the federal deficit. Why? Because that would be the best thing we can do to guarantee a robust economy in the future.

President George Bush

FEDERAL FUNDING OF THE ARTS

The Jesse Helms marketing strategy. Despite the uproar, the Cincinnati show of Robert Mapplethorpe's photography is drawing over 2,500 viewers a day; previous exhibits drew 556 and 225 patrons daily.

TIME

Congress has enough sense to give money to fund art, but they don't have enough sense to know what kind of art they are funding.

The Reverend Donald Wildmon

If we truly believe in decency. . . surely the least we can do is protest the use of taxpayer's money to reward and subsidize utterly filthy so-called art.

Senator Jesse Helms

If America persists in the way its going, and the Lord doesn't strike us down, he ought to apologize to Sodom and Gomorrah.

Senator Jesse Helms

Where does it end? When do these people reach into the Bible and ban the Song of Solomon?

Representative Major Owens

Like trying to catch the grenades as they come over the wall and throw them back before they explode.

John Frohnnayer, Chairman of the National Endowment for the Arts, describing his job

Today the problem with public funds for the arts is not just that subsidies sometimes go to projects in which urinating is important. The problem is that there is no concensus about what art is, or why it is important.

Columnist George Will

THE COURTS

The courts have abandoned civil rights, and now Congress must spend valuable time reaffirming its original intent on these laws.

Representative Don Edwards, on the Civil Rights Act of 1990 which was directed to overturn recent Supreme Court decisions narrowing laws against employment discrimination

If there is anyone who represents the Warren Court's judicial activism, it is Brennan. He is the intellectual leader on the left of the court. Some important cases will go the other way when he is replaced.

Michael Carvin

It is my hope that the Court during my years of service has built a legacy of interpreting the Constitution and Federal laws to make them responsive to the needs of the people whom they were intended to benefit and protect. This legacy can and will withstand the test of time.

Justice William Brennan

The Rehnquist [Supreme] Court has done what no prior court every did. It has decided that decisions that have been on the books for years went too far by providing too much freedom, too much fairness or too much justice.

Clyde D. Leland, Associate Editor, CALIFORNIA LAWYER magazine

Seven of the men are white. Where are the Justices representing the female half of our population and the large percentages that are black and Hispanic? Why has Bush failed to make our court reflect the people it serves?

Ruth H. Collins

I'm sure I've never seen him at a cocktail party, but then, this is a state of recluses.

James E. Duggan, New Hampshire's chief appellate public defender on Supreme Court nominee David H. Souter

ANIMAL RIGHTS

I believe that mink are raised for being turned into fur coats and if we didn't wear fur coats those little animals would never have been born. So is it better not to have been born or to have lived for a year or two to have been turned into a fur coat? I don't know.

Barbie Benton

Madam, do you realize those foxes were anally electrocuted for that coat?

Fur activist Dan Mathews

Animal rights activist: What unfortunate creature had to die for you to get that coat?
A woman: My aunt.

READERS' DIGEST

By next winter, the only practical accessory for a fur coat will be earplugs.

Animal rights activist Dan Mathews

The previous owner of her full-length fox coat was murdered in it, and she is wearing stolen property.

Susan L. Gundich, on women who wear fur coats

Animal rights activist: Do you know how many animals had to die for that coat?
A woman: Do you know how many animals I slept with to get this coat?

Unknown

Hunters have sent me their hunting licenses, tourists have burned their ivory bracelets, doctors support me in my fight against vivisection, and the sale of horse meat in France has dropped by 30 percent.

Brigitte Bardot, commenting on public reaction to her pro-animal campaign

CANDIDATES AND PARTIES

The biggest difference between Republicans and Democrats is that Republicans don't want to raise taxes.

National Republican Congressional Committee
Co-Chair Ed Rollins

Third parties can capture the imagination and affect the agenda and direction of the country.

Eleanor Smeal, on the prospect of NOW's third-party
aspirations

If a third party succeeds, it succeeds because it raises issues so forcefully as to cause significant numbers of people to leave a major party and thus forces that party to address their issues. You don't need a party to do that. Movements do that too. That's what the civil-rights movement did. A third party may not be the best way to do it.

Author Frances Fox-Piven

Measure the man by the enemies he's made.

A slogan for the John Vandecamp campaign for
Governor of California

The perpetual quest for money puts good Democrats figuratively if not literally in bed with the very rich, only a few of whom are in politics for innocent or civic reasons. Too few Democratic elected officials hold on to their progressive values after years in this fund-raising milieu.

Robert Kuttner in THE LIFE OF THE PARTY: DEMOCRATIC
PROSPECTS IN 1988 AND BEYOND

I've always had the feeling I could do anything; my daddy told me I could, and I was in college before I found out he might be wrong.

Ann Richards, Texas governor

I just think we were caught up in the phenomenon of women wanting to put a woman in the governor's office. [It] didn't matter about the qualifications or experience or anything else.

Jim Mattox, former Texas Democratic gubernatorial primary candidate, after his defeat by Ann Richards

In 1988, Americans gave George Bush and Michael Dukakis $46 million each to run their presidential campaigns. If we're going to give them $46 million each, then I think the public should put conditions on how that money ought to be spent. . . .

John Chancellor in his new book, PERIL AND PROMISE

The Fall of Michael Dukakis: How an American Dream Became a Greek Tragedy.

Title of an article in NEWSWEEK

I felt like I had been squashed in a giant compactor.

Kitty Dukakis describing her feelings after her husband's defeat

Any good election lawyer can show you how to get around virtually all the campaign finance laws.

Carol C. Darr, legal counsel

The Congressional campaign system has become toxic with money. We chafe over the burden of having to take our time to go, tin cup in hand, begging to PAC's for the money to run for public office. Yet we have it in our power to stop the madness.

Senator Robert C. Byrd

SOCIAL CONDITIONS

On LBJ Freeway in Dallas, they say, the only way to change lanes is trade cars.

C. Kenneth Orski

As a longtime majority white American, I look forward to the day I become a minority citizen, when I can help form a National Association for the Advancement of White People, receive welfare, demand affirmative action, send my son to college tuition-free and blame all my problems on the nonwhites.

Mary Lou Pearson

There is no greater betrayal than when the earth defaults on the understanding that it stay underfoot while we go about the business of life, which is full enough of perils as it is.

Journalist Jerry Carroll, on earthquakes

We must change the system in our inner cities and pockets of poverty that rewards self-destructive behavior and welfare dependency while punishing individual dignity, initiative, productive work effort, and the family structure.

HUD Secretary Jack Kemp

The theory of America in decline is wrong—dead wrong. In fact, the opposite is true. We are growing to be more prosperous, more creative, more influential in the 1990s then we have been.

Ben J. Wattenberg

The American population that will emerge in the 1990s will be more Catholics, more non-Western, more Mormon, more unaffiliated, and less Protestant than it is today.

George Gallup and Jim Castelli in their book,
THE PEOPLE'S RELIGION

54% of women between the ages of 15–19 have had intercourse at least once.

According to a 1988 survey

The worst and the best hours to drive fall nine hours apart—3:00 a.m. Sunday (most dangerous) and noon Sunday (safest).

According to HEALTH

Older women living outside marriage, especially those who are divorced, experience much lower standards of living than married women.

According to the a study by Teresa Cooney, Peter Uhlenberg,
and Robert Boyd of the University of North Carolina

Americans eat 21,375 acres of pizza per year or 7 1/2 large pizzas each.

U.S.A. WEEKEND

On the Washington beltway police delivered more than a dozen babies last year to women who got stuck in traffic jams on the way to the maternity ward.

C. Kenneth Orski

Single men outnumber single females in their 20s by about 2.3 million, in large part because many women in their 20s have married men over 29.

According to the U.S. Census Bureau

I am disgusted. It's going to affect the beach for years. There will be tar on the beach for years.

Bill Casper, surfer, commenting on the American trader oil
spill off the coast of Los Angeles

About 20% of U.S. high school students have had more than three sex partners and about 3% have injected drugs— putting them at risk for AIDS.

According to a Federal government survey as reported by
Associated Press

College students are more likely to use condoms these days, but otherwise sex habits on campus have changed little since the advent of AIDS.

According to a survey conducted at Brown University

[Economic] growth now depends on the role the city plays in the world market place, not just on the national economy.

John Case

San Francisco County is the most diverse in the nation. The proportion of the five ethnic groups [Asian and Pacific Islanders, American Indians, Hispanics, non-Hispanic whites, non-Hispanic blacks] are closer to being equal there than in any other county in the country.

According to AMERICAN DEMOGRAPHICS

The national concern with pollutants of all kinds—in the atmosphere, the sea, the slums, the movie theaters—trembles on the verge of acute hypochondria, and too many signs point unerringly in the direction of a desperate and intolerant wish to cleanse the world of its impurities. Within the last few years, the agents of the state have taken it upon themselves to examine the citizen rate for flaws in its blood, its urine, and its speech. The media amplify the din of incessant alarm by their ceaseless dwelling on the fear of disease, crime, sin, foreigners, poverty, and death.

Lewis H. Lapham

Overall, a disproportionate number of women, young people, blacks and Hispanics were among the decade's casualties. Even as record numbers of female corporate directors, black millionaires and 26-year-old investment bankers and rock stars were entrenching themselves in upper America, a much larger and growing underclass of high school dropouts, unwed mothers, female heads of households, unemployable black males and homeless persons . . . was beginning to provoke worried citizens about the nation's future.

From THE POLITICS OF RICH AND POOR *by Kevin Phillip*

On any given day, 45% of Americans consume no fruits, and 22% consume no vegetables.

According to the National Cancer Institute

A shopping mall, new office towers, a convention center, an atrium hotel, a restored historic neighborhood. These are the civic agenda for downtown development in the last third of the 20th century, a trophy collection that mayors want. Add a domed-stadium, aquarium, or cleaned-up waterfront to suit the circumstances, and you have the essential equipment for a first class American City.

From DOWNTOWN, INC.: HOW AMERICA REBUILDS CITIES *by*
Bernard J. Freiden and Lynne B. Sagalyn

The median age in the U.S. has risen from 29 in the 1960s to 32. It is projected to reach 36 by the year 2000 and rise into the 40-somethings as we move into the 21st century.

According to Ken Dychtwald in AGEWAVE

In Los Angeles it cost $60,507 to buy what $47,681 buys in Carson City, Nevada.

According to CHANGING TIMES

Communism is collapsing, and just when Americans thought we wouldn't have anyone to hate anymore—the Postal Service is raising stamps to 30 cents.

Joe Hickman

Generational equity is nothing more than the present being fair to the future. Its goal is to pass on our culture, our security, our achievements, and our aspirations, to the next generation—our kids.

U.S. Senator Dave Durenberger

What Ms. Odendahl finds is that the affluent give mainly to preserve elitist institutions that provide pleasure or comfort for the wealthy.

Kathleen Teltsch reviewing CHARITY BEGINS AT HOME *by*
Teresa Odendahl

Thirty-two percent of Americans shop at malls less frequently now than they did a year ago.

According to a poll conducted by Maritz Marketing
Research

Hoosiers are no more anxious to live next to East Coast trash than the residents of the East Coast appear to be.

Senator Dan Coats R-Ind., referring to garbage from New York and New Jersey

CRIME

American children are much more likely to be murdered, live in poverty or come from broken homes than children in the world's other developed nations.

According to a study by the congressional Select Committee on Children

Over 70% of violent crimes committed today are committed by young people under the age of 18.

Jean Dixon, State Representative in Missouri

Over half of all murder victims are related to or acquainted with their killers. At least half of all rape victims know their attacker. The majority of nonsexual assaults are committed by someone known to the victim. Most child molesters are family members, neighbors, teachers, youth group leaders, or other adults who had ongoing contact with children they victimized.

Jennifer Beth Donovan

Life is short; to prove it, criminals sentenced to life get out in ten years.

Gary Apple

Get-tough judges . . . put off to another time and probably for another court the obligation of treating the criminal as something other than a hopeless case.

Columnist Coleman McCarthy

The Insurance Information Institute estimates that fraud [on insurance claims] costs the public up to $15 billion a year.

Richard E. Earley

The Northwest is a particularly attractive area for a serial killer to traverse. . . . That is primarily because of the region's perceived remoteness, its lesser per capita law enforcement and even its reputation for a more laid-back law enforcement.

Head of the Green River Task Force, Capt. T. Michael Nault

In this century, more Americans died in murders than in wars.

L. M. Boyd

Of 187 cities with populations of more than 100,000 Atlanta, Georgia, was the most dangerous city with 3,576 violent crimes per 100,000 people, and Cedar Rapids, Iowa, the least dangerous, with 146 violent crimes per 100,000 residents.

According to an FBI study

Nationally, three deaths daily are attributed to domestic violence. And it is getting worse.

Linda Castrone, Scripps Howard News Service

Current studies indicate that about a third of the women and a tenth of the men in North America are sexually victimized before their mid-teens.

Professor John N. Briere

You are more apt to be killed, injured or physically attacked in your home by someone related to you than in any other social context.

Family violence expert Richard J. Gelles

It takes 51 years of love to do that.

81-year-old Roswell Gilbert, upon being freed from prison after serving 5 years for killing his wife who had Alzheimer's disease

The police really did arrest two Nicaraguans with TOW missiles and an antitank rocket in their pick-up truck, the Miami version of a traffic violation. And a drug enforcement agent really was knocked unconscious when hit in the head with a 200-lb. bale of $20 bills tossed out of a window during a raid.

Journalist Paul Levine

Guns are involved in the deaths of 40% of black male teenagers and 17% of white male teenagers, and firearms are responsible for 11% of all deaths of children under 20 years old.

According to the National Center for Health Statistics

We're seeing a whole generation of young people reacting to two decades of neglect, poverty, and the scourge of the dysfunctional family. The only values they aspire to are survival, power and greed.

John Perkins, of the Foundation for Reconciliation and Development, on urban gangs

Los Angeles is the bank robbery capital of America with 3,300 banks and 1440 heists in 1989. That works out to four bank robberies a day, with an average take of $2,500.

According to FORBES magazine

There is no evidence that juveniles are rehabilitated more readily than others. Aging actually rehabilitates more than any "treatment."

Ernest Van Den Haag

Now that George Bush has made the streets of Panama safe for Americans, I hope he goes on to other things—like making the streets of America safe for Americans.

Joe Hickman, QUOTE magazine

Many well-documented surveys of adults consistently find that 20-40% of adults have a childhood history of at least one sexual-abuse episode. Most often, these adults report that as children they were too frightened or ashamed to tell of the abuse, or that their words fell on deaf ears.

The staff of Children's Charter, Inc.

[Dorothy Rabinowitz] points to events that have become all too familiar to those who have scrutinized the explosion of sex-abuse prosecutions; contamination of child witnesses by "expert" investigators; "scientific" testimony, tailor-made to explain away all contraindications in prosecution evidence; cynical double standards ("believe the children" when their testimony supports the prosecution, reinterpret it when their plain words support the defense); organized community outrage; gutlessness by the press, the bench, and the bar.

Attorney Michael Curtis

A woman is raped every six minutes; every eighteen seconds a woman is beaten; three out of four women will be victims of at least one violent crime during their lifetime.

The Senate Judiciary Committee

There is something inside [serial killers] that is also inside us, and we are attracted to them so we can find out what that something is.

Dr. Ronald Markman

Eighty-five percent of serial killers are men; 82% are white. They like to go after women. The eight percent of serial killers who are female seem to favor poison.

From HUNTING HUMANS: AN ENCYCLOPEDIA OF MODERN SERIAL KILLERS by Michael Newton

An estimated 639,000 Americans are confronted each year by criminals carrying handguns, including 9,200 people who are killed and 15,000 left wounded.

According to a Justice Department study as quoted by AP news service

CAPITAL PUNISHMENT

It is not the responsibility of the government or the legal system to protect a citizen from himself.

Justice Casey Percell

The American system of justice, eloquent in conception and, more often than not, splendid in its actuality, is grotesquely skewed in the so-called capital cases by a barbaric thrust for vengeance rather than justice.

Robert E. Burns

Executing the guilty is a deterrent to crime for that one person.

Benjamin Coats

That was wrong what he did . . . he was way out of line. He could have let those kids go. So I have no pity or compassion for somebody like that. I can't, in good conscience, be in his corner. I can't and if those kids' parents sit there in the front row and clap when he dies I still couldn't sympathize with Robert Harris. I don't want him to live. I want him to die because he killed children.

Convicted murderer Robert Page Anderson, a survivor of three execution dates whose appeal overturned capital punishment in California in 1972

Execute all death row inmates. This will end overcrowding in our prisons.

Tom Neason

The world's first solar-powered electric chair. Now that should satisfy the liberals.

From a cartoon by Carol Simpson

[Capital punishment] demeans and debases us. The death penalty tells our children that it is ok to meet violence with violence.

New York governor Mario Cuomo

The state has to have the right to put mad dogs to death.

Former Atlanta mayor Andrew Young

Why must we kill people who kill people to show that killing is wrong

Sign at a rally against capital punishment

My tax dollars should not be spent feeding, clothing, or caring for murderers, drug dealers, etc. If we can destroy pit bulls, we should destroy society's mad dogs as well.

Judith Ray Legg

Killing doesn't stop killing.
The death penalty is dead wrong.

*Signs at the protest against the execution of
Robert Alton Harris*

Keeping death row inmates alive will increase the chances of solving the problems of murder. By killing them, you erase the answer.

Convicted killer Robert Alton Harris

FAMILY

Once pregnant, white and non-white teens choose abortion at the same rate—approximately 42%.

NEWSWEEK

Nine percent of American women will have had an abortion by age 18; 9% will have had one or more children.

NEWSWEEK

Five million American children under the age of six—almost one of every four in the nation—recently have been in families living below the poverty line.

*According to a national study by Columbia University's
National Center for Children in Poverty*

A greater share of elderly women will be divorcees and they generally will have fewer financial resources than older women who are married or widowed.

*According to a study by Teresa Cooney, Peter Uhlenberg, and
Robert Boyd of the University of North Carolina*

Fifty-four percent of Americans see a parent at least once a week. Sixty-eight percent of Americans talk to a parent on the telephone at least weekly.

According to a Gallup poll

The best cities for raising families:
Tallahassee, Florida
Boise, Idaho
Syracuse, New York
Portland, Oregon
Cedar Rapids, Iowa
Austin, Texas
Omaha, Nebraska
Colorado Springs, Colorado
Stamford, Connecticut
Roanoke, Virginia

According to PARENTING magazine

The average American family will pay $12,938 in federal taxes to cover spending proposed in the 1990–1991 budget.

According to the Tax Foundation

The federal government will spend a family's tax dollar in 1990 in this way: 33 cents for income security, 24 cents for defense, 14 cents for interest, 13 cents for health, 3 cents for education, 2 cents for veterans, 2 cents for transportation, and 9 cents for all other spending.

According to the Tax Foundation

Single men outnumber single females in their 20s by about 2.3 million, in large part because many women in their 20s have married men over 29.

According to the U.S. Census Bureau

Researchers calculated that an average of $4.40 is saved for every public dollar spent to provide contraceptive services to women who might find it difficult or impossible to obtain contraceptives without help.

The Alan Guttmacher Institute

There were more than 4 million births last year, the highest number since 1964.

Cheryl Russel

An estimated 40% of people in their 20s are children of divorce.

TIME

BLACK LIFE

Many [blacks] are fighting to save their families and neighborhoods from the ravages of drugs. Unfortunately, they are almost invisible as far as much of public opinion is concerned.

Drug czar William J. Bennett

Because of continued discrimination, better-off blacks are living next to poor ones in inner-city neighborhoods almost as often today as they did before the civil rights movement.

According to a study by sociologist Douglas Massey

By 1988, one black family in eight had an annual income above $50,000. Twenty years earlier, only one in twenty black families enjoyed an equivalent income.

Robert Lewis

Nationally, 55.3% of black families with children under 18 are maintained by the mother, many of them living in inner cities.

TIME

Large numbers of black professional women are alone, unmarried, and failing to procreate because of the shrinking pool of economically stable or marriageable black men.

Dr. Walter Farrell, Professor of Education
at the University of Wisconsin

Urban black men face a 1-in-10 chance of being killed during their lifetime, compared to a 1-in-80 chance for white men. . . . One of every three black men aged 20-24 who dies is a homicide victim.

Journalist Bill McAllister

Approximately 609,000 African-American males between the ages of 20 and 29—almost 1 of every 4—are either in prison, on probation, or on parole. Comparable figures for Whites are 1 in 16 and for Hispanics 1 in 10.

From a report issued by the Sentencing Project

It's time today—July 8, 1990—to bring it out of the closet: No longer can we proffer polite, explicable, reasons why Black America cannot do more for itself.

Executive Director of the NAACP, Benjamin Hooks

The incessant use of the vocabulary of victimization [by blacks] serves only to sue whites for guilt and to endow blacks with excuses.

Richard A. Oliver

The short-term answer to the black predicament, particularly in the ghettos, is the return of a critical mass of working-, middle-, and upper-class blacks to the inner cities, thus restoring black unity to those communities and fostering and reinforcing interclass mingling.

Kenneth S. Tolletd

EDUCATION

Education is the one investment that means more for our future, because it means the most for our children. Real improvement in our schools is not simply a matter of spending more. It is a matter of asking more, expecting more, of our schools, of our teachers, of our kids, of our parents, and of ourselves.

George Bush in the State of the Union message

Education is the best hope for a drug-free America.

Lauro Cavazos, U.S. Secretary of Education

We are the only country in the industrial world that says to 1 out of every 4 of its young people, we are going to let you drop out of sight, we are not going to give you the tools to be productive.

Former Labor Secretary William Brock

For every dollar spent on a disadvantaged Head Start child, the nation saves six dollars it would otherwise shell out later in the form of additional health, welfare and crime-control expenditures.

Journalist Michael Kramer

Real improvement in our schools is not simply a matter of spending more, it is a matter of expecting more.

President George Bush

Of the 3.8 million 18-year-old Americans in 1988, 532,000 (14%) have dropped out of school, and another 700,000 could not read their high school diplomas.

Roger Rosenblatt

If the health epidemic were striking one-fourth of the children in the country . . . a national emergency would be declared. But when hundreds of thousands of students leave school year-after-year, shockingly unprepared, the nation remains far too lethargic.

Ernest L. Boyer, president of the Carnegie Foundation for the Advancement of Teaching

We may be asking [sex education programs] to accomplish too much. To place the burden of counteracting the prevailing forces in our society towards premarital sex on our schools is both naive and inappropriate.

Drs. James Stout and Frederick Rivara

Senator Ted Kennedy's office released a paper not too long ago claiming that prior to compulsory education, the state [of Massachusetts] literacy rate was 98%, and after that the figure never again reached above 91%, where it stands in 1990.

John Gatto

DRUGS

It is the height of hypocrisy for the United States, in our war against drugs, to demand that foreign nations take steps to stop the export of cocaine to our country while at the same time we export nicotine, a drug just as addictive as cocaine, to the rest of the world.

C. Everett Koop

The "first generation" of children from the 1980s crack epidemic are about to enter public school. They are consistently described as "remorseless," "without a conscience," passive and apparently lacking that essential empathy, that motivation toward cooperation upon which a peaceful and harmonious classroom—and society—so depend.

Michael Dorris

They are impulsive, they tend to act before thinking, they often will tantrum, and may be abusive to themselves, other children without any outward seeming antecedent.

Martin Cavanaugh, Director of Special Education, Mount Diablo Unified School District, on drug, cocaine or crack babies who are now in the schools

The fatal flaw in the policy of prohibition is that those who need to be protected the most—hard-core users—are those least likely to be deterred by laws against drugs.

James Ostrowski

Supply reductions, interdictions, and law enforcement all have failed to curtail drug use. We must bring about fundamand fundamental changes in American values to curb demand if we are to halt substance abuse.

George J. Bryjak

These new addicts are business executives and house painters and doctors and receptionists. And if you met them on the street or at a Little League game, you wouldn't have a clue they're smoking their brains out on crack back home in the basement.

The director of a leading drug treatment center in New York City

Substance abuse is costing the business community $16 billion a year and is responsible for eroding productivity, industrial accidents, absenteeism and tardiness, and inflating health care costs.

Robert M. Stutman

. . . We need to understand that law enforcement is merely a holding operation. We must address the underlying causes of drug-selling and addiction in our society before we can hope for a solution.

Jerome H. Skolnick

The way it must be done is we must generate the programs in which the people, are customers turned away from the drugs, not us turning the drugs away from customers.

Former President Reagan on the nation's drug problems

Young children are going to school with beepers not to connect them to their homes but to their neighborhood drug dealers.

New York Mayor David Dinkins

People view others as if they're TV sets that you can just turn on and switch channels according to your mood. There are lots of exceptions, but there is a definite trend toward the selfish, "hermie" [hermit] approach toward life. That's

why so many people are turning to drugs, because drugs
are also an isolating experience.

> *Professor Povi Toussieng*

White teenagers are more prone to drug addiction than are
Blacks but the media continues to perpetuate the story that
crack is black.

> *Ishmael Reed*

If convicted drug dealers were summarily executed, they
at least would not be back on the streets before the cop
gets his paperwork done.

> *Jo Benzow*

FLAG

It's not a Democrat nor Republican issue. I don't see it as
either liberal or conservative. It's an American issue.

> *President George Bush on the anti-flag burning amendment*

Punishing desecration of the flag dilutes the very freedom
that makes this emblem so revered.

> *Justice William Brennan writing for the majority throwing
> out a Congressional law banning flag burning*

The Congress and the states have power to prohibit the
physical desecration of the flag of the United States

> *The proposed Dole Amendment*

Amending the Constitution to protect the flag is not a matter
of partisan politics. . . It's an American issue.

> *President George Bush*

The integrity of the symbol has been compromised by those
leaders who. . . seem to manipulate the symbol of national
purpose into a pretext for partisan disputes about meaner
ends.

> *Justice John Paul Stevens*

Which is worse, the burning of the flag by some publicity-seeking egomaniac or a well-known member of either political party wrapping himself in the flag?

Clarellen H. Sample

The flag amendment would be the first real instance in which political expression is being suppressed because of objections to the message being communicated.

Duke University law professor Walter Dellinger

Mark my words. It is only a matter of time before someone burns a flag, calls it "kinetic art" and gets a great grant to take his act on the road.

Columnist George Will

There is something wrong when our national leaders would rather debate how to save the fabric of our flag rather than the fabric of our people's lives.

Mayor Art Agnos

For heaven's sake, the strength of the republic transcends any perceived threat from a handful of goofy flag-burners . . . . At worst, these attention-getters should be ignored for their bad manners.

Martin Keating

If Congress wants to ban flag-burning, there's no reason to go to the extreme of passing a constitutional amendment. Congress can just pass a law requiring that all American flags be made from flame-retardant material.

John P. Markey, Jr.

READ MY LIPS . . .

The Congress will push me to raise taxes, and I'll say no, and they'll push, and I'll say no, and they'll push again, and I'll say to them, "Read my lips: no new taxes."

Presidential Candidate, George Bush, 1988

The President has kept his promise your GNU will not be taxed.

NATIONAL REVIEW

If there is one thing that can bind the conservative movement together—if its not the threat of the Soviet Union—would be George Bush reneging on the one campaign pledge everyone remembers and that really distinguishes conservatives from liberals.

Heritage Foundation analyst Stuart Butler

The T word.

Reference used in Washington for taxes when President Bush became president

Apparently he was saying "No new Texans" and he's kept that promise.

Unknown

Read *my* lips: No more Bush.

Lori A. Spackey

We know from reading Bush's lips that he talks from both sides of his mouth.

Robert Borosage

Read my lips: I was lying.

David Letterman

The world read my lips but my lips were crossed.

THE CAPITOL STEPS

AND SO FORTH

Five states with the lowest median age:
Utah, Alaska, Wyoming, Louisiana, Mississippi.

Five states with the highest median age:
Florida, New Jersey, Connecticut, Pennsylvania, New York.
According to the U.S. Bureau of the Census

Compared to natives, [immigrants'] rate of participation in
the labor force is higher, they tend to save more, they apply
more effort during working hours, and they have a higher
propensity to start new businesses and to be self-employed.
Julian L. Simon in THE ECONOMIC CONSEQUENCES OF
IMMIGRATION

Americans live in a celebrity culture. At home they are in
constant search of heroes, while abroad they are on the
lookout for supervillains—tyrants and aggressors whose in-
disputable nastiness makes it easier to comprehend why so
much of the outside world often seems an unfriendly if not
dangerous place.

Strobe Talbott

The top five small cities:
1. San Luis Obispo-Atascadero, California
2. Corvallis, Oregon
3. Fredericksburg, Virginia
4. Fairbanks, Alaska
5. Wenatchee, Washington

According to THE READING GUIDE TO LIFE IN AMERICA'S
SMALL CITIES *by G. Scott Thomas*

The number one injury suffered by women in the United
States happens in the home.
According to the JOURNAL OF THE AMERICAN
MEDICAL ASSOCIATION

A home is being seized or abandoned every two minutes
in the USA. States with the highest percentage of home
mortgages: Alaska, Oklahoma, Wyoming, Colorado, Louisiana.

As reported by USA TODAY

The youngest baby boomers turned 26 this year.

Cheryl L. Russel

A few weeks ago, Kristina and I were given tickets for this play. . . . We left here at 5 in the afternoon. The play starts at 8:30. . . . We didn't even hit Long Beach until 8 because of the traffic. . . . We turned around. We went bowling instead.

LA Rams quarterback, Jim Everett, on life in LA

Defaults on student loans will cost taxpayers about $2 billion this year. Of the $51 billion lent to students since 1965, $7.8 billion is in default.

According to the Department of Education

Industrial and infrastructure decay are the threat to U.S. National Security.

Professor Seymour Melman

Percentage of householders who own their own home—68%.

CAMBRIDGE REPORTS TRENDS AND FORECASTS

Chapter 3

THE WORLD

MANDELA/SOUTH AFRICA

I went to jail 27 years ago, couldn't vote. Today, 27 years later, I can't vote.

Nelson Mandela

Mr. deKlerk himself is a man of integrity who was acutely aware of the dangers of a public figure not honoring his undertakings. But as an organization [the African National Congress], we base our policy and strategy on the harsh reality we are faced with, and this reality is that we are still suffering under the policies of the nationalist government.

Nelson Mandela

Whites are fellow South Africans, and we want them to feel safe and [to know] that we appreciate the contribution they have made toward the development of the country.

Nelson Mandela

We are trying to convince the white minority that it is madness that we should be killing one another when we can sit down, talk, and settle our problems.

Nelson Mandela

I have fought against white domination, and have fought against black domination. I have cherished the idea of a democratic and free society in which all persons live together in harmony and have equal opportunities.

Nelson Mandela

Mandela is out of jail but not free. Not free to move to the neighborhood of his choice. Not free to send his children to the school of his choice. Not free to vote. Not free to run for office in his own country.

Jesse Jackson

Mandela was not a prisoner of conscience. Nelson Mandela was tried in 1954 for sabotage and treason. At the trial, Mandela admitted that he had planned sabotage.

David Howard

Our struggle has reached a decisive moment. We call on our people to seize this moment so that the process toward democracy is rapid and uninterrupted. We have waited too long for our freedom. We can no longer wait. Now is the time to intensify the struggle on all fronts.

Nelson Mandela

Nelson Mandela is far from the paragon of virtue that many envision. He is, in fact, responsible for the deaths of many innocent people, black and white, who died as the result of his instigation of bombing public places, like railway stations, where people who were blown to bits did not have a chance to voice their beliefs or fight for equality.

Gertie Taylor

The world will be watching as we edge, apprehensively, towards reconciliation. That same world should also examine its own conscience. . . . If sanctions ever served their useful purpose (which we doubt) they should be reconsidered.

THE JOHANNESBURG SUNDAY TIMES

President F.W. deKlerk did what many people have yearned for such a long time. He did what is right for our children and grandchildren.

THE JOHANNESBURG RAPPORT

If they really believed they were better, would it be necessary to create laws guaranteeing social, monetary, and political superiority?

South African Jai Bhula, on the white minority

The season of violence is over. The time for reconstruction and reconciliation has arrived.

South African president F.W. de Klerk

You've got to understand, in this country the blacks are the best treated in the world. We build hospitals, we build schools, we build colleges. And who pays for it? The white man. And then they go and burn the things down because of their disputes. I'm not being racialistic when I say this but I think you must be fair.

South African Robin Cochrane

What oversea's people don't realize is that the black man is not interested in politics.

South African Guy Hart

Mandela and deKlerk are like turkeys. They won't live to see Christmas.

South African Funnie Meyer

INVASION OF PANAMA

When the United States decides by itself who is going to run a country, it runs the risk of ending up running the country itself.

Richard Nixon on the Panama invasion

Because of what our people did there, Panamanians will live in freedom.

Ronald Reagan

I applaud the President's strong action.

Gerald Ford

I deplored the invasion and feel a great responsibility now for our nation to help repair the damage caused by U.S. economic embargo and our military action

Jimmy Carter on the Panama invasion

The American Santa Claus came to Panama in the camouflage uniform of a marine.

PRAVDA

Soviet president Mikhail Gorbachev has renounced interventionism. George Bush has done exactly the opposite. He claims the right to intervene in the internal affairs of a sovereign nation and to dictate the terms of its political life.

Carlos Fuentes in EXCELSIOR *of Mexico City*

Every once in awhile, the condescension of the U.S. toward Latin America reaches dizzying new heights. . . . Virtually all Latin states are glad to be rid of General Manuel Noriega but the egregious excesses committed by the U.S. To accomplish its goal has simply reinforced Yankee imperialism run amok.

The TORONTO STAR

What really scared Noriega out? The troops began to play "Wayne Newton's Greatest Hits!"

Walt Handelsman

You're no good.

Title of song played by occupying American troops outside the Vatican embassy where General Noriega took refuge

If Dante were designing a hell for him that is what he would do. No cocaine. No pornography. No little boys—just a bunch of nuns and priests.

> *Richard Koster on Noriega's asylum at the Vatican*
> *embassy in Panama*

Gen. Noriega could prove a tougher adversary in court than he was in the streets of Panama city. . . . Apparently, American law will be a more effective weapon [for Noriega] than was his saber.

> *Henri Pierre in* LE MONDE

An overkill onslaught, unleashed on the pitifully weak high in state so as to bring down a tin-horn dictator whom we helped bring to power.

> *Hobart Rowen, commenting on the Panama invasion*

To a great extent, the intervention in Panama was an acknowledgement of U.S. Inability to manage this crisis politically. It is not that peaceful means were exhausted but that the U.S. has never been capable of using them.

> *Antonio Cano in* EL PAIS *of Madrid*

The president is riding high on a wave of public approval, and the decision to use force to drive Noriega from power has finally erased his long-standing image as a hesitant, weak president. Not since World War II have the American people seen television images of their "boys" in a land where the people greet them with hugs, kisses, and flowers.

> *Jochen Siemens in the* FRANKFURTER RUNDSCHAU

NICARAGUA

After ten years of trying to destroy Nicaragua, we do have a responsibility to help democracy.

> *Senator Patrick Leahy*

I wish I could feel as proud of my country as the people of Nicaragua felt of their revolution which after ten years of U.S.-imposed strangulation, they have finally been forced to give up on . . . for now.

Robert Bollan

The great significance of the stunning electoral defeat of president Daniel Ortega's communist dictatorship is that America has brought democratic freedom to Nicaragua as it brought it to Eastern Europe, has started bringing it to the Baltic states, and will I believe eventually bring it to the Soviet Union.

William Randolph Hearst, Jr.

No one said democracy was cheap.

Congressman Dante Fascell on aid to the new Nicaraguan government

A change of government does not mean the end of the revolution.

Former Nicaraguan president Daniel Ortega

Nicaraguans are not different than most people. They don't want their children to starve or their sons to die in war. And so they voted not so much for Violeta Chamorro, but for the hope that a Sandinista defeat would bring an end to the U.S. policies that have brought them so much suffering.

Jan Bowman

We will rule from below.

Former Nicaraguan president Daniel Ortega

I would rather be thought of as a Latin Margaret Thatcher.

Nicaraguan president Violeta Chamorro

EASTERN EUROPE/PERESTROIKA

It is in the interest of the U.S. to see perestroika succeed.

President George Bush

. . . It's like wartime Britain.

Sean Connery, on the Soviet Union

Fanatics in Moscow have revived the bogus protocols of the Elders of Zion, and claim that Adolf Eichmann was in fact a Jew, conspiring to rule the world. In Hungary, the Star of David was plastered on the campaign posters of a party deemed to be led by Jews. In Poland, where few Jews remain, tens of thousands took to the streets to demonstrate for a "Jew-free Europe." In Rumania, there is talk of purging the sacred national soil of the polluting blood of Jews and Magyars.

Ian Bururma on anti-semitism in Eastern Europe

Take a look at what's happened in Eastern Europe. These people, some of them went out there in the streets and got beat up pretty bad just because they wanted to do something as simple as vote. And here you would have to take people out in the street and beat them up pretty bad to make them vote.

Frank Zappa

The children and grandchildren of the leftist radicals who put Russia through the meat grinder in pursuit of socialist happiness want to do the same thing in the interest of capitalism.

Editor Stanislav Kunyayev

At the general strike in Prague in late November [1989], Zdenek Janick, a Czech brewery worker, climbed up on a platform, looked out at his audience and recited the following: "We hold these truths to be self-evident, that all men are created equal . . ."

LIFE

Mikhail Sergeyevich [Gorbachev] must know that he cannot win the race with history, that it is beyond the wits of one individual or the lifetime of one man to communicate his vision and alter all the road maps and guide a whole new generation to the other side of the abyss. It appears that what he's trying to do is smash as many walls of the past that he can, so the enclosure that has separated his country from the community of developed western nations can never be reassembled.

Gail Sheehy

Comrades, this man has a nice smile but he's got iron teeth.

Andre Gromico, trying to assure the Soviet old guard that Gorbachev was tough and shrewd. From the book GORBACHEV: HERETIC IN THE KREMLIN

The deeper meaning of the overthrow of communism is the realization that man can shape neither history nor society by five-year plans.

Columnist Charles Krauthammer

We have no alternative but to keep members of the party in their jobs—they are our civil servants. Without them the country would collapse.

From one of The Front leaders

What the revolutionaries want is leaders who are "savvy, intelligent, and do not at all compromise"—in other words, "people who don't exist in Romania."

From a former U.S. embassy official

The casino, perhaps the ultimate symbol of capitalist decadence, has invaded the Soviet union: Casino Moscow has opened on an experimental basis.

Kitty McKinsey

We must combine the best of capitalism and the best of socialism. Capitalism is certainly effective, but with socialism you do not work too much, and this is an advantage that needs to be preserved.

Lech Walesa

The train of German unification is moving so fast, that at times it seems to have arrived before departure times have been announced.

Werner Holzer

To pass from democracy to dictatorship takes only one day, but to pass from dictatorship to democracy takes many more.

Romanian Prime Minister Petre Roman

By no means do I want to topple the government; I just want to stick a pin in its back side so that it picks up the pace a little bit. I do not want to cause it any harm.

Lech Walesa

Now that democracy is replacing communism in Eastern Europe, it means the end of elections that are rigged—and the beginning of elections that are bought.

Joe Hickman, QUOTE magazine

I think it's great that you're trying to bring America to Czechoslovakia.

Cab driver to an American businessman

In your country [U.S.] you struggle so the poor will be rich and in our country we struggle so the rich will be poor.

Andrei Brezhnev, grandson of Leonid Brezhnev

We are very disappointed. Ceausescu is gone, but so many old faces will remain. We did not fight for this.

A young Romanian on his new government

The reason for Mikhail Gorbachev's economic difficulty should be apparent. The stick of a command economy disappeared in the Soviet Union during the past several years, but the carrots of a market economy have not yet grown.

Anders Aslund

Any attempt to coerce or intimidate or forcibly intervene against the Lithuanian people is bound to backfire. That is inevitable.

President George Bush

Democracy is the fundamental aim of political life.

New Romanian president Ion Iliescu

Where else can you study capitalism and get paid for it?

Oleg Mukhin at the new McDonald's in Moscow

I like waiting for a newspaper. For the first time here, there's news worth reading about.

A Bucharest undergraduate

It has been destroyed by the will of peoples who wished no longer to tolerate coercion.

Edward Shevardnadze, Soviet foreign minister, commenting on the end of the communist monopoly in Eastern Europe

This is a city after a heart attack.

Warsaw resident after the collapse of the socialist economy

[Roumania is] a nation based on natural selection. Only the strongest and toughest can get on our crowded buses. The older people remain in the cold. We will have trouble establishing true democracy in this climate.

A Romanian student

You can't just turn a tank factory into a car factory. Besides, as we try to revive this economy, we'll need all the hard currency we can get.

Czechoslovakian industry expert on the dilemma facing his country's military production capacity

The communists may be gone, but they have locked us into a web of arms deals and even terrorism that may be impossible to escape.

A Czechoslovakian interior ministry official

Propaganda is always a ratings loser. Night after night of paeans to "the genius of the Carpathians" can convert even the most ardent communist into a skeptic.

Jonathan Alter

Perestroika has already awakened our people. They've changed. We have a different society now. We will never slip backward. We will keep moving ahead.

Mikhail Gorbachev

If, in any area of Soviet foreign policy, we're doing something that damages the interests of the U.S., then that policy cannot be successful.

Mikhail Gorbachev

To be a communist, as I see it, means . . . through political action, to help working people realize their hopes and aspirations and live up to their abilities.

Mikhail Gorbachev

To exercise self-determination through secession is to blow apart the union, to pit people against one another and to sow discord, bloodshed and death.

Mikhail Gorbachev on Lithuania and other
secession-minded republics

It is a question of who has sovereignty over this land. Does it belong to the people of Lithuania or to some other state?

Lithuanian president Vytautas Landsbergis

Stay on the footpath. We don't know if they took away all the mines.

East German mother to son as they cross over to West Berlin

They want gadget socialism, video tapes, microwave ovens, computers, all kinds of gadgets.

Gus Hall, chairman of the Communist Party U.S.A., on changes in East Germany

The good news is I saw Gorbachev in the supermarket. The bad news is he took the last 36 cans of pork and beans.

Wife to husband in a cartoon by Stayskal

There is no halfway house between communism and democracy.

Richard Nixon

The revolution has come. But what are we to do? We must rebuild the whole country. Where do we begin?

Romanian citizen

We're supposed to smile all the time—people will think we have gone looney!

Oleg Mukhin, one of the 630 people hired to run the first McDonald's in Moscow

People don't care about all the new [political] parties. They just want to buy things.

Anonymous East Berliner commenting on the explosion of freedom behind the Iron Curtain

Political parties? We don't know anything about them. They have certain platforms, but in my opinion they are not good. They talk and talk. . . . They talk too much.

Romanian factory worker Irinel Ricu

IRAQI INVASION OF KUWAIT

He wants people to be afraid of him because he feels that is how you get respect.

Near East expert Barry Rubin on Iraqi president Saddam Hussein

Saddam is very isolated and paranoiac. Part of the reason for the foreign invasions are his own internal problems.

Strategic analyst Shireen Hunter

No memos were required. It was all in his head. He operated exactly opposite of how Reagan worked. He knew the military thrust should follow the diplomatic. He knew that to be effective, the line-up against Saddam had to be perceived as more than just the rich west against a poor Arab.

A Bush aide

It is not often that the world produces a dictator who so blatantly disregards the laws of civility to commit such an overt, unambiguous act of aggression against a peaceful neighbor that poses no security threat whatsoever. It is rare that a victim's fortunes are so directly tied to the health of the western economies. And it is more unusual that the aggressor rules an all but landlocked country dependent on imports for food and on the sufferance of its neighbors to get its one significant income earner, oil, to market.

Journalist Lisa Beyer

America is being held hostage not only by Iraq, but also by Detroit.

Because, according to Daniel Becker, Detroit is building bigger and less efficient cars

It's not profiteering. It's prudence.

Henry Schuller, energy-security expert on the quick rise in oil prices after the Kuwaiti invasion

Why should young Americans die just so that we can drive gas guzzlers?

William P. Garvey

I cannot remember a time when we had the world so strongly together against an action as now.

Prime Minister Margaret Thatcher on the Iraqi invasion of Kuwait

Standing up for our principles will not come easy. It may take time and possibly cost a great deal.

President Bush on the Iraqi attack on Kuwait

Pentagon orders double up the night before the Panama attack; same thing happened before the Grenada invasion. [Last Wednesday, before Iraq's surprise invasion of Kuwait] we got a lot of orders, starting around midnight, we figured something was up.

Washington, D.C., Domino's Pizza delivery runner

If they push this guy [King Saddam] too hard, bombs will go off in Europe.

Noel Koch, counterterrorism expert

The real significance of this crisis is that it is going to divide the post-cold war world.

A senior Bush administration official

Soviet support for our position totally disoriented the Arab states. Suddenly, they couldn't hide behind the superpower conflict. They had to step up to the issues themselves.

A U.S. diplomat

The aim is to destroy Iraq's war-making potential and to inflict such damage . . . that the Iraqi military will overthrow Saddam.

A Pentagon official

Read My Ships

Title of TIME story on President Bush's reaction to the Kuwait invasion

We have no troops there [in Saudi Arabia]. We are not preparing troops and there is no talk about this. But if we are asked to participate with Arab troops, I do not think Egypt would refuse.

Egyptian president Hosni Mubarak

Sending U.S. military forces to Saudi Arabia will cost an estimated $300 million to $440 million dollars a month.

As reported by Associated Press

The mission of our troops is wholly defensive. Hopefully, they will not be needed long. They will not initiate hostilities, but they will defend themselves, the kingdom of Saudi Arabia and other friends in the Persian Gulf.

President George Bush

Please don't write that Moslems are doing this to Moslems. Saddam isn't a [true] Moslem. If the Israelis invaded they would treat us better than this.

A Kuwaiti woman

We would rather die than be humiliated, and we will pluck out the eyes of those who attack the Arab nation.

Iraqi president Saddam Hussein

The first army came to fight, the second army has come to loot.

Nagiba Diaball of Kuwait

It was like hell. The Iraqis are taking the food. People are fighting each other for food.

Mrs. Al-kandry of Kuwait

Iraq attacks Kuwait, there's an upheaval in Liberia, there's an attempted coup in the Philippines. . . . You get the feeling that the Goodwill Games just didn't work out this year?

Comedian Jay Leno

AND SO FORTH

Chinese communists have this view that only after the liberation of the whole world can one liberate oneself. But I believe that if each person would liberate themselves first, then the world could liberate itself.

Shen, Chinese youth

The only law that the narco-terrorists do not break is the law of supply and demand.

Columbian president Virgilio Barco

I am driving a packed bus at 150 km per hour, headed for a cliff. Either we put on the brakes and some people get a little bruised up, or we go over the edge and we all die.

Newly elected Brazilian president Fernando Collor de Mello's evaluation of the economic situation in his country

If there is one place in the world where as secretary of defense I get up in the morning worried about the possibility you could have a short-warning or a no-dash notice attack against U.S. forces, it is in Korea.

Defense secretary Dick Cheney

[Prime Minister Thatcher] will not be there forever. She is mortal. She has much heart, but all hearts stop. However, she does resemble that gruff Englishman, who when he suffered palpitations, would thump his chest and bellow "go *on*, go *on!*" until his heart obeyed. She intends to go on and on.

Columnist George F. Will

Art collectors are expected to bid 50 million dollars for a Renoir oil painting. It's not high when you consider how expensive oil is these days.

Gary Apple

Japan Now Ahead In Nuclear Power, Too.

Headline from THE NEW YORK TIMES

[Princess Diana] is prepared to make sacrifices to maintain her position, the main one being marital happiness. If she was in love with Charles once, I don't believe she is now.

A palace source

Royals aren't supposed to show emotion. [Princess Diana] is totally different from all that. Probably shaking hands with an AIDS patient is the most important thing a royal's done in 200 years and she is going to shake hands with a leper in Indonesia next month.

Judy Wade

Diana has to turn a blind eye to the fact of how incredibly selfish Charles is. . . . He expects everybody to kowtow to him, to bow and scrape, and he has tried to treat his wife in the same way.

A close observer

Total number of children, grandchildren, and great-grandchildren born to the average American woman—14; born to the average African woman—258.

According to WORLD MONITOR

Mideast arms purchases from the United States in the past decade: Israel—$5,582 million; Saudi Arabia—$19,308 million

According to the Defense Department

Ever since the beginning of my presidency, I have been convinced that much of the terrorism, human suffering, and even the potential genesis of a third world war lies in the unresolved Israeli-Palestinian conflict.

Former President Jimmy Carter

By a majority of at least four to one, American Jews wanted some formula that would quell the violence in the West Bank and the Gaza Strip. Two-thirds favored some form of political accommodation with the Palestinians.

Robert Spero

Why are people so fascinated by American arrangements?
... The answer is simple: sooner or later they expect American arrangements to be theirs.

Senator Daniel Patrick Moynihan

Queen Elizabeth's personal jewelry, not including the
Crown Jewels, is worth at least $57 million.

According to the LONDON DAILY MAIL

Chapter 4

BUSINESS

MARKETING

We, the great believers in free enterprise, are having our pants removed, an inch at a time, by a centrally orchestrated, totally committed, economic aggressor. Why can't we grasp the truth of it? And get mad and fight back? Or don't we give a damn anymore?

Chrysler Motors Chairman Bennett E. Bidwell
on the Japanese

The trick is to watch what the winners are doing. Copycat marketing may be tough on your creative ego, but it is easy on your pocketbook.

Jack Falvey

[R.J. Reynolds'] "Uptown's" message is more disease, more suffering and more death for a group already bearing more than its share of smoking-related illness and mortality.

Secretary of Health and Human Services on R.J. Reynolds'
plan to market "Uptown" cigarettes to blacks

If we were Sears developing a line of clothing for blacks, this would pass without any notice.

R.J. Reynolds' spokeswoman

Instead of fancy engineering or complicated management strategies, quality actually boils down to something quite simple—serving customers, serving them in such a way that they keep coming back. . . . What the scandals of Boesky, HUD, the pentagon, Milken boil down to is the simple fact that a lot of people were serving only themselves.

Forsythe Group's vice president Ralph Brauer

The mass market essentially is dead. Instead of the nuclear family, we have live-alone singles, live-together singles, adults living with adult children, two-career parents with or without kids, and mine-and-yours families.

Professor Richard Feinberg

Western hopes of a stable and increasingly affluent China buying huge quantities of foreign products, seem more remote today than they did a decade ago. China is likely to remain a relatively poor country for a long time . . . If there ever is truly a huge, unified China market, it will likely be captured not by the foreigners who have been pursuing this commercial dream for more than a century, but first of all by the Chinese themselves.

Author Jim Mann in BEIJING JEEP: A SHORT, UNHAPPY
ROMANCE OF AMERICAN BUSINESS IN CHINA

You have this *thirtysomething* generation that's very interested in building a better baby. Books are an accepted way to do it.

Nancy Pines, marketing director for kids' books at Bantam

At a time when overall economic growth is crawling along at 2%, spending on and by kids 4–12 years old jumped an estimated 25% last year to $60 billion. This year the kiddy market is expected to hit $75 billion, approaching 2% of the entire U.S. economy.

Peter Newcomb

Companies are marketing pajamas with kitschy motifs, making them the hottest bedroom trend since lace lingerie. The pajamas are littered with fish or golf balls or dollar signs or ducks or even little piggies.

> *From the* MARIN INDEPENDENT JOURNAL

We all would accomplish more with older people if we generally ignored age per se in market place communications. The consumer behavior of older people, especially in terms of discretionary spending, is influenced far more by levels of maturity than by a person's age.

> *Author David Wolfe in* SERVING THE AGELESS MARKET

They don't want anything that makes them think ugly, or really, makes them think period. It's right to the orgasm—no foreplay at all.

> *Bill Cosby, who has just helped produce a new jazz album, talking about record companies and their lack of desire to take a chance on someone new*

One billion packs of cigarettes are sold annually to children under 18 years of age.

> *According to the* JOURNAL OF THE AMERICAN MEDICAL ASSOCIATION

Teens spent $71 billion on products and services for themselves and their families in 1989.

> *According to Peter Zollo of Teenage Research Unlimited*

ADVERTISING

It holds six big gorgeous men. This is something I like in a car.

> *Tina Turner, in a commercial for Plymouth Acclaim*

Travel with the airline that has room for your two most important carry-ons. Your legs.

> *Airline commercial*

Today fur. Tomorrow leather. Then wool. Then meat . . .
Ad campaign by the Fur Information Council of America

Equity, sweet equity.
An advertisement for home equity loans by Wells Fargo Bank

The flavor of America. It's the way you live, the things you do, the tobacco you chew.
From an ad for Redman chewing tobacco

Joey's big sister went to school on the GI Bill. Now Joey's signed up.
From an ad for the U.S. Armed Forces

Life's basic necessities. Food. Shelter. Lee jeans.
From an ad for Lee Jeans

Sneakaroma.
Used in commercial for Keep It In Your Sneakers

Remember it's the ability not the disability that counts.
Motto of the Rose Resnik Center

Color has power. Research suggests weightlifters actually lift less in pink rooms.
From an ad for Cycolor paper

You're watching a woman save an animal's life.
Advertisement for B.W.C. cosmetics

The mayor reckons I'm like a glass of warm milk. I help all of Georgetown get a good night's sleep.
Larry Adkins, Georgetown fire chief, in a Toyota ad

Gordon's—for a new gin-eration.
Billboard advertisement for Gordon's gin

Boycott Folgers coffee. What it brews is misery and death.
TV ad, narrated by Ed Asner, accusing Procter & Gamble of prolonging the 10-year civil war in El Salvador by buying Salvadoran coffee beans

New York Life—The company you keep.
From an advertisement for New York Insurance Co.

America West. What we serve is you.
Slogan for America West Airlines

She makes my knees weak, so I chose a diamond that takes her breath away.
From an advertisement for Lazare Diamonds

The party is over.
Advertisement for Vodka in the Minneapolis area featuring a picture of Gorbachev drinking vodka

Lazyboy. The name America's comfortable with.
Lazyboy commercial

The perfect recess.
Advertisement for Parliament Lights

Fahrvernugen [driving pleasure].
Slogan used in the Volkswagon advertisements

In life I have always been bachelor #4.
From a K-Mart commercial

I say our cars are every bit as good as Japanese cars, but nobody knows it.
From a commercial featuring Lee Iacocca

Now credit is the same price as cash.
Slogan for Chevron advertisement

When your hair's right, everything's right.
> *From a commercial for Agree Shampoo*

Can't beat the real thing.
> *New Coca Cola slogan (Old slogan: "It's the real thing")*

Nothing Beats a Bud.
> *The new 1990 slogan for Bud beer replacing*
> *"This Bud's for You"*

Tampax tampons: Biodegradable since 1936.
> *Tampax T.V. commercial*

They hardly show the car anymore in ads. . . . Why should they: They all look alike. So it's all lifestyle and feel-good stuff.
> *Tom Magliozzi of "Car Talk"*

Advertising, not its audience, is manipulated, to serve the audience's emotional needs.
> *Columnist George Will*

Vamping with the brothers.
> *Advertisement for Christian Brothers Brandy in an all black*
> *neighborhood featuring all black models*

What makes Teri Garr feel good? Fruit of the Loom panties.
> *From an advertisement for Fruit of the Loom*

Super-Maxi-Thin-Mini-panty liner.
> *Ad for Stayfree thin pads*

I knew she had simple tastes. So I made sure her diamond was simply incredible.
> *Ad for Service Merchandise*

He's crazy about my kid. And he drinks Johnny Walker.
> *From an advertisement by Johnny Walker*

A face is like a work of art. It deserves a great frame.

Ad for L. A. Eyeworks sunglasses

This is not your father's Oldsmobile.

Line from Oldsmobile commercial

A friend of mine says she has better luck in chosing her lingerie than in choosing her dinner companions. Perhaps there's just a better selection of lingerie out there.

From a Maidenform advertisement

Is two months salary too much to spend for something that lasts forever?

Ad for Service Merchandise

Bo knows.

Popular T.V. commercial

The freshness should not leave one's mouth as soon as one's toothbrush does—The Colgate Wisdom Tooth.

From an ad for Colgate toothpaste

It's so beautiful we're afraid some people will miss the point.

Advertisement for the new Parker Duofelt Bull Point Pen

The BMW 325i convertible. The ultimate tanning machine.

Ad for BMWs

Live sports coverage is one of the best advertising environments you can create. It's real, dramatic and wholesome.

ESPN President Roger Werner

The sneakers of winners shouldn't smell like losers.

Dr. J. Irving for Dr. Scholl's Sneaker Snuffers

If we all aged half as well, the world would be a much more civilized place.

Advertisement for Ballantine's scotch

Don't be stupid, stay in school.

New commercial for Nike shoes

Quaker Oat Squares. You're going to love them from Square One.

Advertisement for Quaker Oat Squares

Some men have higher aspirations than others. That's why you seek the finest life has to offer. And why you wear shoes from Johnston & Murphy.

Ad for Johnston & Murphy shoes

All dressed up. And someplace to go.

From an ad for Luvs Deluxe diapers

Put your principal where your principles are.
You can do well by doing good.

Slogans from socially responsible investment funds

Violent toys . . . may, in fact, teach children to become more violent.

Line from an ad for Dakin Plush Toys

Richer than an OPEC nation.

From an ad for new Chips Ahoy! Selections cookies that was cancelled during the Kuwaiti crisis

Not for the meek or insignificant.

Advertisement for Chivas Regal

SAVINGS & LOAN CRISIS

I saw a senator on one of those Sunday morning talk shows the other day and he said that the actions of the Senate have created a lot of jobs for a lot of citizens.
Yeah, but, let's face it, you can't make a career out of jury duty.

Comedian Jay Leno on the Keating Five

The amount needed to bail out insolvent savings and loan institutions is said to be $200-300 billion or even higher. ... We cannot recapture the lost funds, but we can make sure that the S & L debacle does not happen again.

George J. Benston

[Helping financier Charles Keating was] not unlike helping the little lady who didn't get her Social Security.

Senator McCain

I would be a coward and a wimp if I said to a contributor ". . . I won't help you" for fear of appearing improper.

Senator Alan Cranston

In hindsight I think the Savings & Loan security cameras should have been pointed at the managers instead of the customers.

Gary Apple

If someone would have told me that the day of the bill signing that the S&Ls would be the number one issue then the crisis would look even worse than it did a year ago, I would have said "you're crazy."

Rep. Charles Schumer, one year after President Bush signed the savings & loan bailout law

It is rooted in the explosion of constituent service as the mainstay of a Congressional office—and the impossibility of clearly distinguishing between such service and outright favoritism.

Mark B. Liedl on the savings & loan scandal

The S&L bailout represents the first root of an unprecedented experiment in laissez-faire economic theory. Deregulation of the nation's savings & loan industry under Presidents Jimmy Carter and Ronald Reagan transformed the nation's primary public policy mechanism for generating affordable housing for all classes of Americans into a one trillion dollar, federally insured gambling casino, where unscrupulous insiders became show winners—with the gov-

ernment-guaranteed license to steal—and the only sure losers seem to be U.S. taxpayers who get to pay for a world-
class play that they were never invited to attend.

Journalist Curtis J. Lang

Except for the taxpayers . . . nobody took the slightest risk.

Lewis H. Lapham on the savings & loan scandal

The moderate economic growth of the last years has suc-
cumbed to an orgy of speculation—junk bonds, leverage
buy-outs, S&L's—a casino economy where the high rollers
keep raising the stakes, confident that the taxpayers would
cover the losses.

Robert Borosage

If a fraction of the billions spent on bailing out the savings
and loan industry were diverted to diverse (and daring)
art activities, Americans would be a rich and much enriched
people.

Laura B. Mersky

AND SO FORTH

The [Rolling] Stones aren't playing rock'n'roll any more.
They are playing for Budweiser.

Singer Mike O'Connell

They say I'm a witch with a "b" on the front. It's the age-old
problem. Someone else would be called a shrewd businessman. Women are called other things.

Singer Anita Baker

The best real-estate investments with the highest yields are
in working-class neighborhoods, because fancy properties
are overpriced.

Jane Bryant Quinn

Right off the plane I fell into 35 photographers. All Japanese. They were probably taking pictures of my luggage so they could copy it smaller and cheaper.

Michael Caine, after a recent flight

Where most tourists to America come from:
1. Canada
2. Mexico
3. Japan
4. United Kingdom
5. West Germany

According to the U.S. Travel and Tourism Administration

The worse the economy, the higher the rate of divorce.

Psychologist Howard Markman

Most adults pass through three life stages and each stage helps to determine the kinds of experiences they will seek as consumers. Young adults crave "possession experience" during the career and family-building years. Their satisfaction comes from establishing their status, so they seek to own a nice house and fill it with objects. After those needs are satisfied, consumers develop greater interests in "catered experiences" such as travel, education, or sports. Finally, adults will seek "being experiences." This is an anti-materialistic stage when people derive the greatest satisfaction from simple pleasures and human contact.

According to David Wolf in SERVING THE AGELESS MARKET

The most visited cities by tourists to America:
1. New York City
2. Los Angeles
3. San Francisco
4. Honolulu
5. Miami
6. Washington, D.C.

According to the U.S. Travel and Tourism Administration

Last year Phillip Morris sold 318 billion Marlboro cigarettes. That's equal to about 60 cigarettes for every man, woman, and child on earth.

According to the UNIVERSITY OF CALIFORNIA, BERKELEY WELLNESS LETTER

Ethics is the moral strength to do what we know is right, and not to do what we know is wrong.

C.J. Silis, Chairman Phillips Petroleum

Of 1000 manufacturers surveyed, 217 invested overseas last year. Over half of the investments were in the European Community.

According to the Conference Board

Profits from Japanese companies have slowed more abruptly than anyone expected. Pre-tax profits have deviated from 27% in the first quarter of 1989 to 8% for the first quarter of 1990.

According to the ECONOMIST

Best therapy I know. Make some money, feel better.

From a cartoon by Weber

In my experience, failures provide the lessons to ensure progress, and success breeds self-confidence. Failures are important because they shorten the learning curve for others to follow.

Nihachiro Katayama, Chairman of Mitsubishi Electric

Many start-up firms concentrate on creating the future without successfully managing the present.

Harry S. Dent, Jr.

The top five U.S. Banks:
1. Chemical Bank & Trust Company, Midland, Michigan
2. Davenport Bank & Trust Company, Davenport, Iowa
3. Farmers & Merchants Bank, Long Beach, California
4. First National Bank of Anchorage, Alaska

5. First National Bank of Clearwater, Florida
According to BANKING SAFETY DIGEST

More than 4.5 million women in the U.S. are sole proprietors of small businesses.
Sharon Nelton, commentator

People can be label-conscious, but the quality of my clothes is as high as that of the top designers.
Jaclyn Smith, on her K Mart clothing line

American business can out-think, out-work, out-perform any nation in the world. But we can't beat the competition if we don't get in the ball game.
President George Bush on investment in Eastern Europe

Bedside manners are no substitute for the right diagnosis.
Peter Trucker quoting Alfred Sloan

The best U.S. business schools for management:
Harvard University, for marketing
Northwestern University, for production management
University of South Carolina, for finance
The University of Pennyslvania, for human resources
Massachusetts Institute of Technology, for international business
According to U.S. NEWS & WORLD REPORT

The top five business franchises:
1. Restaurants
2. Retailing (non-food)
3. Hotels, motels, and campgrounds
4. Business aids and services
5. Convenience stores
According to the International Franchise Association

The five most entrepreneurial cities:
1. Las Vegas, Nevada
2. Washington, D.C.

3. Orlando, Florida
4. Tallahassee, Florida
5. San Jose, California

According to INC.

Frank Lorenzo demolished Eastern Airlines, wreaked havoc on thousands of worker's lives and severely devalued Continental Airlines. Our condolences to whatever industry he stalks next.

John Peterpaul, V.P. of the International Association of
Machinists and Aerospace Workers

Ten megatrends for the 1990s:
1. The booming global economy
2. A renaissance in the arts
3. The emergence of a free-market socialism
4. Global lifestyles and cultural nationalism
5. The privatization of the welfare state
6. The rise of the Pacific Rim
7. The decade of women in leadership
8. The age of biology
9. A religious revival of the new millennium
10. The triumph of the individual

According to John Naisbitt and Patricia Aburdene in
MEGATRENDS 2000

The five hottest real-estate markets in the U.S.:
1. West Palm Beach, Florida
2. Akron, Ohio
3. Greenville, South Carolina
4. Mobile, Alabama
5. Sacramento, California

According to U.S. NEWS & WORLD REPORT

I transgressed certain of the laws and regulations that govern our industry. I was wrong in doing so and knew at the time, and I am pleading guilty to these offenses.

Deposed junk-bond king Michael Milken

The five biggest automakers in the U.S.:
1. General Motors
2. Ford
3. Chrysler
4. Toyota
5. Honda

> *According to Integrated Automotive Resources'*
> FAST TRACK NEWS

Somebody said to me, "But the Beatles were anti-materialistic." That's a huge myth. John and I literally used to sit down and say, "Now, let's write a swimming pool."

> *Paul McCartney*

The "post-it" has bolted into the Big Four of office-product sales along with file folders, tape and copier paper.

> *From* THE SUNDAY TIMES

Feat of Clay

> *Title of article on Clamation founder William Vinton*

The fall of Drexel-Lambert is a symbol of the end of the 80's which was the decade of debt. We simply borrowed too much at every level.

> *Andrew Tobias*

It was really set up like a big corporation. You walked into their office— with computers and work stations. It looked like an automated travel agency.

> *Paul Seidel, Deputy District Attorney, commenting on the*
> *break-up of the biggest prostitution ring*
> *in the country, Cloud 9*

Sommaire.

> *Name for the first computerized air bed which has a micro-computer to adjust air into eight balanced pressurized cylinders that support the sleeper's weight*

Niche Programming.

> *An effort by T.V. networks to target narrow demographic groups by focusing shows*

The 1980s were to debt what the 1960s were to sex.

James Grant of GRANT'S INTEREST RATE OBSERVER

We have it all over Japan. We have the richest mix of ethnic groups and global experience. The richness of this mix yields America's incredible creativity and innovation.

John Naisbitt

The future isn't what it used to be.

Gerrit Jeelof, commenting on the shifting European business situation

Interest on the [national] debt is a $179 billion social-welfare program for owners of capital, who tend to be conservatives.

Michael Kinsley

Nothing confers freedom like a buck in the bank.

Business tycoon Malcolm Forbes

There isn't going to be anyone after dark any more in Times Square if these buildings are all filled with law firms and advertising agencies, unless these young warriors are waiting at midnight for their stretch limos to take them home to Scarsdale.

Brendan Gill, on the proposal to build four massive office buildings on Time Square

I will tell you a secret: Dealmaking beats working. Dealmaking is exciting and fun and working is grubby. . . . Dealmaking is kind of romantic, sexy. That's why you have deals that make no sense.

Peter Drucker, on hostile takeovers

Under the plan, called HeartGuide, food manufacturers submit their products to be analyzed for cholesterol, salt, and total and saturated fat content. Items that meet the American Heart Association's approval would be allowed to use the seal on labels and in advertisements.

Widely touted plan that was rapidly withdrawn

There has been a shakedown in the fast food business because, when it began, it made some promises to the American public. It was supposed to be fast, inexpensive, prepared quickly, and offer a limited menu that could stand relatively long holding periods. The fast food organizations have broken their promises.

Professor Joseph Durocher

Nearly 6,000 people are placing their faith—and money— *Psychic Forecaster*, a monthly newsletter that uses psychics to chart the future of the economy and the market.

NEWSWEEK

Of the 1070 alumni of the [Columbia University Business School] from the classes of 1953 through 1987, 40% said they have been implicitly or explicitly rewarded for taking some action they considered to be ethically troubling. Thirty-one percent of those who refused to take some ethically troubling action said they had been penalized for their choice.

As reported in the WALL STREET JOURNAL

Deregulation is dead as a national political issue. What you're going to see in the next decade is a lot of reregulatory fine-tuning.

Marvin Kosters of the American Enterprise Institute

Overall, one of the main legacies of the Reagan era has been erosion of American competitiveness. . . . Mr. Reagan did not appear to recognize the problem despite the rising trade deficit and reliance on foreign capital. Instead he focused on the immediate prosperity.

Peter Riddell

Chapter 5

HEALTH

FOOD

McDonald's, Your Hamburgers Have Too Much Fat!

> *An ad placed in several papers by Phil Sokolof of Omaha, Nebraska, an industrialist and an anti-cholesterol crusader*

The fat in these [tofu-based] burgers is mostly unsaturated, good for the heart, maybe, but not for one's weight.

> *Jayne Hurley of the Center for Science in the Public Interest*

The ultimate behavior-modifying tax would be placed on calories. Look at the economic and social benefits: less over-eating, fewer fat people burdening our health-care systems.

> *W. Scott Moore*

Foods aren't good or bad. Eating habits are.

> *From an ad by the American Heart Association*

Old Food Label
  Calories
  Carbohydrates
  Saturated Fat

Additions proposed by HHS Secretary Louis Sullivan
   Calories from Fat Proteins
   Cholesterol Sodium
   Dietary Fiber Fat

There's no healthy food. Healthful food, yes. You're healthy, if you eat, but it's not.

From a letter to columnist L.M. Boyd

By 1995 people will be ordering ostrich burgers.

Melodye Crawford

People are munching on chemicals every time they eat microwave pizza, popcorn, waffles, and any other product that uses packaging to brown or crisp food.

Lisa Lefferts of the Center for Science in the Public Interest

Natural carcinogens in meat, grain and other foods are a far greater danger than pesticides and additives, accounting for more than 98% of the cancer risk in the diet.

According to Dr. Robert Scheuplein, director of the Office of Toxicological Sciences, U.S. Food and Drug Administration

Most granola cereals are more like dessert than breakfast fare. Though they usually contain whole grains, they also pack lots of fat . . . and sweetness.

UNIVERSITY OF CALIFORNIA, BERKELEY WELLNESS NEWSLETTER

I tell kids they should throw away the cereal and eat the boxes . . . At least they'd get some fiber.

Dentist Richard Holstein

A weekly serving or two of fish can greatly lower chances of suffering a fatal heart attack. Test subjects who ate fish benefitted more than patients on two other commonly recommended heart-healthy regimens: high-fiber and low-fat diets.

According to the UNIVERSITY OF CALIFORNIA, BERKELEY WELLNESS NEWSLETTER

Vegetables do not contain all of the amino acids, or protein-building blocks, necessary to form complete proteins, which are essential for building muscle and keeping the blood, brain and other organs healthy. Also, iron is not absorbed as easily by the body when it comes from vegetable sources.

*Mindy Hermann of the American
Dietetic Association*

The best fast-food meals:
1. McDonald's chicken salad oriental
2. Burger King's chicken salad
3. Jack-in-the-Box chicken fajita pita
4. Carl's Jr. BBQ chicken sandwich
5. Taco Bell's bean burrito with green sauce
6. Hardee's grilled chicken sandwich

*According to the Center for Science in the
Public Interest*

The worst fast-food meals:
1. Hardees Big Country Breakfast [sausage]
2. Jack-in-the-Box ultimate cheeseburger
3. Taco Bell taco salad with shell
4. Arby's roast chicken club sandwich
5. McDonald's McChicken sandwich
6. Taco Bell taco light

*According to the Center for Science in the
Public Interest*

The most popular ice cream flavors:
1. Vanilla
2. Chocolate
3. Butter pecan
4. Strawberry
5. Neapolitan
6. Chocolate chip
7. French vanilla

According to the International Ice Cream Association

Raw garlic inhibits blood clotting and may be a better heart-attack preventer than aspirin.

According to researchers at the Pharmacology Department of Tulane Medical School

Eating lots of garlic may: (1) lower bad cholesterol and raise good cholesterol levels, (2) prevent heart disease by increasing the time it takes blood to clot, and (3) prevent and possibly reverse the early stages of atherosclerosis.

According to NUTRITION ACTION HEALTHLETTER

If you knew how meat was made, you'd probably lose your lunch.

k. d. lang

Beef consumption is down 4%, pork consumption is down 14%, poultry consumption is up 28% and seafood consumption is up 20%.

According to the Department of Agriculture

DIET

The most miserable thing is giving up champagne and caviar.

Robin Leach, commenting on dieting

Women gained 6 to 7 pounds and men added 3 to 4 pounds in the past decade.

According to studies in Minnesota and Rhode Island

American dieters made an average of three attempts to lose weight during the past year.

According to the Calorie Control Council

Reducing your saturated fat intake by 5% will lower your blood cholesterol 3 times more than if you reduce your cholesterol intake by the same percentage.

According to Dr. John LaRosa of the American Heart Association

Decaf coffee—but not regular coffee—raised cholesterol levels in a study of 180 middle-aged coffee drinkers.

According to the Stanford University Medical Center

Among people over age 59, those who ate the most fruits and vegetables had 25%-40% fewer fatal strokes than those with lower potassium intakes.

According to a NATURAL HEALING NEWSLETTER

People believe in better living through chemistry. They would rather take a pill than stay away from cheeseburgers and shakes.

Dr. Jerry Avorn

Adding 100 grams of oat bran to the daily diet produces a 7.5 percent drop in serum cholesterol, but so does ordinary low-fiber wheat flour and cereal.

According to the NEW ENGLAND JOURNAL OF MEDICINE

Be wary of a widely publicized recent study which claimed that oat bran doesn't lower cholesterol levels. The study was based on insubstantial research which virtually guaranteed oat bran would fail to lower cholesterol.

According to MEN'S HEALTH NEWSLETTER

Of 1088 children those who regularly ate a morning meal had lower cholesterol levels and weighed less than those who started the day without food.

According to researcher Ken Resnicow

If you try to lose much more than a pound or two a week, you're setting yourself up for failure. You might lose twenty pounds initially but you will gain it back with a bonus.

Dr. Ronna Kabatznick

The thinner any woman is for her height and age, the less likely she is to have a heart attack or other heart disease.

According to a study published in the NEW ENGLAND JOURNAL OF MEDICINE

The prime time to ward off weight gain is in one's early 20s. Twenty-five to thirty-four-year-old men gained almost twice as much as men aged 35-44, and women between 25-34 gained nearly 50% more than women ten years older.

According to a study from the Centers for Disease Control

You have what we call a natural food problem. If there's food around, you just naturally gravitate toward it.

From a cartoon by Mugs

Men who spend three hours of day in front of the tube have doubled the rate of obesity than those who discipline themselves to exercise less than an hour a day.

According to a study from Auburn University

Obesity is a major cause of heart attacks in women. The risks of obesity have been underestimated and underappreciated.

Dr. Joann Mantz

The most effective way to keep off the weight you just lost from dieting is to add exercise to your routine, rather than to continue your reduced calorie intake.

According to TUFTS UNIVERSITY DIET & NUTRITION LETTER

College educated men are on average 2-3 lbs. heavier for their height than men who didn't make it past high school.

According to COSMOPOLITAN

By far the most serious addiction in the United States is to food. It is impossible to determine the exact mortality rate as a result of people's dietary habits, because most often dietary excesses kill not directly, but by causing some ailment such as heart, kidney, or circulatory failure.

Herbert Berger, M.D.

The top three diet book best-sellers:
1. *The Hilton Head Metabolism Diet*
2. *The T-Factor Diet*
3. *The Rotation Diet*

B. Dalton Bookseller

I can't postpone my life until I lose weight. I have to live right now.

Delta Burke

Fully 40% of women, but only 19% of men, feel guilty about snacking between meals. Peak snacking time is in the late evening.

According to a survey by Continental Baking Co.

DOCTORS

These are tranquilizers . . . take two before reading my bill!

Cartoon by Stayskal

The average patient sits in a doctor's waiting office for eighteen minutes after arriving for an appointment. The best appointments for the shortest waits are the first one in the morning and the first after the doctor's lunch break.

According to the American Medical Association

Well, Bob, it looks like a paper cut but just to be sure let's do lots of tests.

Doctor to patient in a cartoon by Mankoff

About 50% of the physicians said patient demand was their main reason for prescribing medication.

According to a study at the Harvard Medical School

I had a video taken of the operation. The doctor said it was the best movie I ever made.

Shirley MacLaine, about her recent knee operation

Physicians and dentists are more than twice as likely to commit suicide than any other male occupations.

Associated Press

ALCOHOL AND TOBACCO

Researchers have generally estimated that about 5,000 non-smokers a year get lung cancer from the tar and nicotine in other people's cigarettes. The new study . . . suggests that 46,000 non-smokers may be dying annually from exposure to tobacco smoke in the air.

Paul Raeburn

Smoking costs the nation more than $52 billion a year, largely for health care expenses.

*According to a report by the Department of Health and
Human Services*

Smoking cigarettes that are relatively low in tar and nicotine does not reduce the risk of heart attacks.

*According to a study by the Boston University School
of Medicine*

Cigarettes Kill.
Tobacco Is An Addicting Drug.
Cigarette Smoke Harms Non-smokers.

Proposed new warning labels for cigarettes

The vast majority of people who have ever used illicit drugs, such as marijuana and cocaine, had previously used cigarettes and alcohol. . . . Conversely, people who have never smoked only rarely abuse illicit drugs or alcohol.

*Results from a survey at the National Institute
on Drug Abuse*

By the turn of the century, smoking will be the foremost cause of death throughout the world.

> *According to a World Health Organization study*

Mothers who smoke at home increase their kids' chances of developing asthma.

> *According to a study from the Boston University School of Medicine*

Among the periodicals that ban cigarette ads are: *Business Week, The New Yorker,* and *The Nation.*

> *According to* HEALTH

Utah has the lowest proportion of smokers (18%). Kentucky has the highest percentage of smokers (38%). Maine has the highest percentage of former smokers (20%).

> *According to a federal survey*

Although public service advertising provides some of television's most powerful imagery, the gut-wrenching scenes of tearful teenage alcoholics or drug-overdose victims shrouded in black body bags are not persuading people to make long-term changes in their behavior.

> *The results of a study by the Harvard School of Public Health*

Alcohol is responsible for more than 100,000 deaths annually in the United States, stealing 2.7 million years from drinker's lives.

> *According to federal health officials*

A hard-drinking daddy can cause [fetal alcohol syndrome] even if mom doesn't drink at all.

> *According to Dr. Robert A. Anderson, Jr., who has studied fathers for twelve years*

Only one or two alcoholic drinks a day may enlarge your heart and increase your risk of heart failure.

> *According to the National Heart, Lung & Blood Institute*

Alcohol, a legal drug, kills more people each year than cocaine, an illegal drug.

William R. Wilder

Women are so comfortable saying, "I'm a recovering addict, the problem is in me." They are so uncomfortable saying the F word: "I am a feminist; the problem is also in society." Women get much more support when they define their problems in medical rather than political terms.

Therapist Harriet Learner

More than 3000 teenagers become regular smokers each day.

According to Dr. Antonia Novello

AIDS

The man of my dreams is a rubberman.

Ad for condoms for AIDS

I use to feel that I needed to score with others to have a good time . . . until I realized I was putting my family at risk.

From an AIDS poster

If you get the AIDS virus now, you and your driver's license could expire at the same time.

From an AIDS poster

Eleven years is the average incubation period of AIDS among homosexual and bisexual men infected with HIV.

According to the San Francisco Department of Health

I tend to trivialize the men. There are either women trapped in men's bodies, like Alan Alda and Phil Donahue, or younger guys who are like camp followers looking for easy lays. Those males don't vote and when they do, they're starry-eyed liberal democrats who subscribe to Playboy.

Representative Robert Dornan about men who support abortion rights

Massachusett's 1990 income-tax returns will include a check off allowing filers to contribute to AIDS programs.

Scott R. Schnedel

Linda Kean, 36, a heroin user and prostitute, suspects she got the [AIDS] virus from a contaminated needle. She hasn't felt any symptoms yet—and she doesn't tell customers or other hookers in Oakland that she is infected. That, she says, would be "professional suicide."

NEWSWEEK

Today, AIDS is the most common cause of death among those 25–44 years of age in New York City.

According to the NEW ENGLAND JOURNAL OF MEDICINE

AIDS has become the most privileged disease in America. Why? Mainly because its victims are young, in many cases creative and famous. Their deaths are therefore particularly poignant and public.

Columnist Charles Krauthammer

Talk is cheap. AIDS funding is not.

Sign carried at the President's speech on AIDS

Three hundred thousand dead from AIDS. Where is George?

Chant at the International AIDS Conference

40.7% of gay and bisexual men from 20 to 24 who were treated in sexual-disease clinics were infected with the AIDS virus.

According to a study quoted in TIME

For those who are living with HIV and AIDS our response is clear. They deserve our compassion. They deserve our care. And they deserve more than a chance—they deserve a cure.

President George Bush

We can all grow and learn in our lives and I've learned that all kinds of people can get AIDS, even children. But it is the disease that is frightening, not the people who have it. You can't catch AIDS from hugging someone. I am not asking you to send money; I am asking for something more important—your understanding.

Public Service Announcement by former president
Ronald Reagan

Once disease strikes, we don't blame those who are suffering. We don't spurn the accident victim who didn't wear a seatbelt. We don't reject the cancer patient who didn't quit smoking. We try to love them and care for them and comfort them. We do not fire them or evict them or cancel their insurance.

President George Bush in a speech on AIDS

Prevention is still better than cure and, for the most part, AIDS is a preventable disease. It is not stopped by street marchers and demands.

Joanne Wulf

We are fighting a deadly disease. We're not fighting the people who have it or the people we think who might have it.

Former Surgeon General C. Everett Koop on AIDS

ABORTION

By criminalizing abortion even for cases of rape and incest this society would send a clear message that any man, under any circumstances, has the right to force any woman to bear his children.

Tandy Y. Cook

I read your story on the U.S. Supreme Court's decisions upholding state requirements that pregnant teenagers notify parents or a judge before having an abortion. Let me see if I have this straight. A pregnant teenager notifies a judge of her desire to have an abortion. The judge interviews her. If the judge decides she is sufficiently mature, she may have the abortion. If the judge decides she is too immature to make such a decision, she must become a mother. The logic entirely escapes me.

Margaret C. DeVault

Fighting abortion on strictly political grounds will not produce a morally acceptable solution unless the language of reverence and sanctity becomes familiar to both the electorate and the elected.

Lynn Crydernan in an editorial in CHRISTIANITY TODAY

If the clash of absolutes is a clash between life [the life of the fetus] on the one hand, and liberty [that of a woman] on the other, solutions that split the difference—denying some fetus's life and some woman's liberty—offer no solution.

Lawrence H. Tribe, ABORTION: THE CLASH OF ABSOLUTES

The quality of birth control in the United States is not likely to change by the year 2000, with the consequent likelihood that there will be no significant reduction in the number of abortions . . . Indeed, contraceptive choices in the United States at the end of the century may be even more limited than they are now.

Professor Curl Djerassi, "the father of the pill"

Much opposition to abortion seems really to be about the control of women.

Lawrence H. Tribe, ABORTION: THE CLASH OF ABSOLUTES

Teenage girls are 24 times as likely to die of childbirth as of a first-trimester abortion.

According to the Alan Guttmacher Institute

Rape and incest are tragedies, but why visit on the second victim, the unborn child . . . capital punishment.

Illinois Congressman Henry Hyde

DEATH WITH DIGNITY

With abortion we deny the time to be born, and with our increased medical technology we deny the terminally ill the time to die. Surely it is "a time to weep."

Jeanne Joyce Williquette

The Kevorkian; The Suicide Machine.
Names given to the intravenous device developed by a doctor (Kevorkian) in Michigan and used by a woman Alzheimer's patient (J. Adkin) to kill herself

It's not death with dignity to have to travel 2000 miles from home and die in the back of a camper.

Derek Humphry, Founder of the Hemlock Society on Jane Adkin's use of the Kevorkian machine

I'm trying to knock the medical profession into accepting its responsibilities, and those responsibilities include assisting their patients with death.

Dr. Jack Kevorkian, who designed the suicide machine

Physicians are not supposed to be exploiting patients for their own benefit, and that's what he did.

Alexander Capron, Professor of Law, Medicine and Public Policy

Either the rights to live and to die are both sacred, or neither is.

Treska Lindsey

The right to die must include the right to choose to die, so that death can be a blessing when life has become a curse.

Reverend Ralph Mero

The obligation of the physician to the comatose, vegetative, or developmentally disabled patient does not depend upon the prospect for recovery. The physician must always act on behalf of the patient's well-being.

The Association of American Physicians and Surgeons, in a
brief to the Supreme Court

It is difficult to answer such questions, but all but two of us believe that it is not immoral for a physician to assist in the rational suicide of a terminally ill patient.

Twelve prominent physicians in the NEW ENGLAND
JOURNAL OF MEDICINE

[If euthanasia were permissible] a patient could never be totally confident that the doctor was coming to help him and not kill him.

George Annas, director of Boston University's Law, Medicine
& Ethics Program

ENVIRONMENT

Top 3 Wastemaker Awards to:
Coca Cola Company for packaging its Minute Maid juice in non-recyclable boxes wrapped in plastic;
Eastman Kodak Company for its single-use Fling camera;
Colgate-Palmolive Company for Fab One Shot laundry detergent.

According to an organization of environmental activists

We know what the public doesn't yet know—degradable plastics don't disappear, they are not a real and long-lasting solution.

Carl Kamena of Dow Plastic in a 1989 memo

We were startled to uncover this rate of global deforestation. We were saying we were losing the forests at an acre a second, but it is much closer to an acre and a half a second.

World Resource Institute President James Gustave Speth

We have survived without the whaler and the buffalo hunter. What's the big deal about losing the old-growth logger?

Douglas W. Briggs, Jr.

The landscape has been so transformed by ignorance, arrogance and greed that those who must prove their case are not those who call for forest protection, but those who call for business as usual.

Richard Brown of the National Wildlife Federation

We survived without the dinosaur. What's the big deal about the [spotted] owl?

Bruce Goetsch

I LOVE SPOTTED OWLS . . . FRIED.

T shirt

To put it bluntly, we don't know what the hell is going on. . . . We're being blackmailed and threatened from both sides. Industry is saying "Support our side, or you'll lose your jobs." Environmentalists are saying "Support our side, or you won't have clean air to breathe." People are scared to death.

Lonnie Burson, lumber- and millworkers union leader

I reject those who would ignore . . . the economic consequences of the spotted owl decision. I also reject those who do not recognize their obligation to protect our delicate ecosystem. Common sense tells us to find a needed balance.

President George Bush

People and planets before profit.

Sign at Earth Day rally on Wall Street

It is the earth that endures. All of us are only tenants in stewardship of a sacred trust.

President George Bush

The spotted owl could prove to be a blessing if it forces Oregon to rebuild its economic base.

Laurie D. Greene

AND SO FORTH

Something in me began to sing . . . it was more than a resurrection. It was a creation. Adam the second day in the garden: I was going to stay.

A. C. Greene in TAKING HEART, *describing his feeling after a heart transplant*

Music seems to touch handicapped kids on a deeper level. It makes them calmer and more relaxed.

Curt Smith

Life is like a B-grade movie. You don't want to leave in the middle of it, but you don't want to see it again.

Ted Turner talking about dying in his sleep the way that Malcom Forbes did

The long-awaited five-year study found "no evidence" that Agent Orange injured soldiers in the field. The report did conclude that Vietnam veterans are more likely than the general population to get a rare, fatal cancer called non-Hodgkin's lymphoma.

Andrew Purvis

Reagan Administration officials "obstructed" an Agent Orange exposure study in Vietnam veterans.

According to a report of the House Committee on Government Operations

A howling tempest in the brain.

William Styron's description of depression

Chronic emotional distress and anxiety during pregnancy importantly contributes to premature births and low birthweight babies, independently of other medical risks.

Psychologist Marci Lobel

If you pick up any current actuarial table and look up the average lifespan for a person of your particular age, sex, and weight, you'll realize that, statistically, you have to squint like hell to read the numbers.

Dave Barry in DAVE BARRY TURNS 40

Thanks to jogging, more people are collapsing in perfect health than before.

SUNSHINE MAGAZINE

The annoyance the man might feel at being forced to wear a condom is nothing compared to the fear the woman might feel were he not to use one.

Sydney Biddle Barrows

Health care expenditures . . . are estimated to soar to $2 billion *a day* by 1992.

Harvey C. Sigelbaum

Home health care will grow by more than 12% annually over the next five years, making it the fastest growing area in the entire health care industry

Charles Laverty of Curaflex Health Services

Probably the most common addiction [to non-prescription] drugs would be to laxatives, especially with older patients.

Professor Charles Seifert

Containers used in microwave cooking could be releasing potentially harmful substances into our food.

According to the Center for Science in the Public Interest

Statisticians say divorce is three times more likely than the national average among couples with one partner who is arthritic.

L. M. Boyd

Most wanted plastic or cosmetic surgery for women: Liposuction, breast augmentation, collagen injections, and eyelid tucks. For men: nose jobs, eyelid tightening, liposuction, tummy tucks.

According to the American Society of Plastic and Reconstructive Surgeons

The risk of cancerous tumors and leukemia from radiation is 3-4 times higher than previously estimated.

The National Research Council of the National Academy of Sciences

The people will see themselves in a negative light, positive light events threaten self-concept.

Psychologist Jonathan D. Brown

An aspirin a day may actually reverse the effects of dementia [mental deterioration] that is caused by poor circulation.

According to MEN'S HEALTH

Depressed people tend to accept only negative feedback, which reinforces their negative feelings about themselves.

Victoria M. Esses

Twice as many adults have been tested for cholesterol levels in the past year than in the previous year, with 1 out of 3 now knowing their level.

According to Gallup polls

I compare skin damage [by the sun] to a taxi meter. If you're fair-skinned, your meter runs faster than if you're dark-skinned, although in either case you can't make the meter go backwards.

Dr. Darrell Rigel of New York University Medical School

Emotional factors are often more important than the joint damage in determining pain and impairment in arthritis. An attitude that a disease is hopeless tends to lead to disability. On the other hand, people who see their disease as threatening, but also look for ways to cope, tend to do better.

Kristofer J. Hagglund

Accidents are a major cause of death among youngsters. A simple approach like teaching a child to be careful of traffic and keeping hazardous materials in your home out of kid's hands can save lives.

Dr. Gunnard B. Stickler

Vitamin overdose in children under six ranks among the top ten calls to poison-control centers.

According to Nurse Rose Ann Soloway

Men with known coronary artery disease are susceptible to increases in angina attacks and EKG abnormalities when they exercise in atmospheres with high carbon monoxide levels.

According to a study published in the
NEW ENGLAND JOURNAL OF MEDICINE

Noise affects more Americans than any other pollutant.

According to Joseph J. Soporowski

Ultrasound is being put to work on broken bones. The technique helped heal wrist and leg fractures within six weeks— compared to an 8-to-12-week healing time among people who didn't use ultrasound.

According to a study reported by
Peter D. A. Warwick

A key to helping a child cope with an illness is to involve her in some aspect of treatment.

Cynthia Hoppenfeld Rosin

The most successful woman dieters are those who had a degree of self-confidence, great motivation, low levels of job stress in their lives, and a well-developed social support system.

According to a study by Nutri/System

Honey is extremely thick, and this, along with its antibiotic properties, enable it to absorb water from swollen tissue, clean the wound, and protect it from further infection.

Dr. Alimuddin Zumal of Hammersmith Hospital in London
on the curative abilities of honey

There is no evidence that these devices [walkers] help children learn to walk faster, but the devices do make it easier for them to get into dangerous situations.

Dr. Fernando Mendoza

If parents talk about or care for a child in a way that communicates that she is weak, frail and sick, the child will see herself as weak, frail and sick.

Dr. Gerald Koocher

Of 86 women with terminal metastatic breast cancer, those who took part in a weekly group session lived an average of 37 months—18 months longer than those who received no psychological therapy.

According to a study by Dr. David Spiegel

The ten most common causes of death for Americans.
1. Heart disease
2. Cancer
3. Stroke
4. Accident
5. Lung disease
6. Pneumonia and influenza
7. Diabetes
8. Suicide
9. Chronic liver disease and cirrhosis
10. All other causes

According to the National Center for Health Statistics

People in a negative mood were much more likely to believe negative feedback.

Victoria M. Esses reporting on a study of 50 undergraduates

Humor that puts down authority figures is most strongly related to illness risk among men. For women, unhealthy laughs come from self-deprecating jokes and humor that centers on anxiety.

According to Dr. James Carroll, professor of psychology

There is only one-third as many colon cancer deaths in New Mexico as in New Hampshire, and older people who move from New York to Florida experience a reduction in their risk of colon cancer. This suggests that sunshine [our largest source of Vitamin D] may help prevent colon cancer.

According to NUTRITION ACTION HEALTHLETTER

The disease of the 90's: Borderline Personality Disorder. Impulsive and self-destructive, feeling chronically empty or bored, becoming frantic over the thought of abandonment, having sharp mood swings, feeling uncertain about your self-image.

According to SELF

In a study of 30 women who had fat suctioned from their thighs, abdomen and hips, 16 experienced breast enlargement 6–12 months after the procedure. Five women gained enough fullness to require a larger bra.

Laura Flynn McCarthy

Women whose breast cancer surgery was performed during the middle of their menstrual cycle suffered no recurrence of cancer. Women whose surgeries were performed at other times of the month had at least a 40% relapse rate.

According to a study by Dr. William J. M. Hiushesky

For at least 20 million Americans, chronic pain is a daily torment. . . . Some of the most common causes are arthritis, back problems, cancer, headaches, facial pain, nerve damage, spinal cord injury and burns. Of all types of chronic pain, low back pain is the most common.

According to the MAYO CLINIC HEALTH LETTER

Some contemporary eponyms:

The Huckleberry Finn syndrome—the tendency to play hookey from school and work.

The Cinderella Complex—women who yearn to be taken care of.

The Peter Pan Syndrome—men who refuse to grow up.

The Snow White Syndrome—a woman's fear that she won't be liked if she is too successful.

The Delilah Syndrome—sexual promiscuity caused by fear and dislike of a domineering father.

The Ostrich Complex—people who try to escape their problems by hiding from them.

The Sunglass Syndrome—cold-like symptoms caused by pressure of too-heavy sunglasses.

The Frankenstein Syndrome—contradictory feelings about knowledge and power

From the book MEDICINE, LITERATURE AND EPONYMS
by Dr. Al Rodin

Seven warning signs that indicate a medical emergency:
1. Chest pain or upper abdominal pain or pressure
2. Difficulty in breathing or shortness of breath
3. Fainting or feeling faint
4. Dizziness, sudden weakness, or sudden change in vision
5. Sudden severe pain anywhere in your body
6. Severe or persistent vomiting
7. Suicidal or homicidal feelings

According to the American College of Emergency Physicians

The bottom line on the public's attitude is: Spend whatever is needed for health care—particularly on me—just don't bill us for it.

Richard Morin

A man spends the first half of his life learning habits that shorten the other half.

Ann Landers

9.7 of every 1000 babies died before their first birthdays, down from 9.9 in 1988.

> *According to the National Center for Health Statistics*

A baby born in 1989 can expect to live 71.8 years, up from 71.4 the previous year.

> *According to the Metropolitan Life Insurance Co.*

A muscle is like a car. If you want it to run well early in the morning, you have to warm it up.

> *Florence Griffith-Joyner*

I avoid the sun. Sunshine is actually fatal. There's a plan to cover the earth with a gigantic squeeze tube of sunscreen with a sun-protection factor of 17. Until then, it's not a good idea to go outside, not to look at the sun on television or even to hum, "Here Comes the Sun."

> *Dave Barry, on the secret of living past 40*

There is no prescription for growing old. But when you work hard, you get hard and go on living.

> *Centenarian Sarah Silvers*

You probably aren't middle-aged until you think more about past events than the future.

> *Statement chosen by 47% of respondents in a poll*
> *on middle age*

What we are talking about is a loss of control and willingness to risk any kind of consequence for a pleasure that gets you so hooked you cannot stop.

> *Psychologist Patrick Carnes describing sexual addiction*

Pain is the body's way of informing the mind that we are doing something wrong, not necessarily that something is wrong.

> *Norman Cousins*

I thought my wife was just forgetting things. Then she forgot my name.

Advertisement for the Alzheimer's Association

Researchers have identified for the first time a gene that may predispose some people to alcoholism, giving credence to the idea that alcoholism is a disease rather than a behavioral problem and raising the possibility of new methods of prevention and treatment.

Journalist Janny Scott

I was on the stump all the time exhorting young people to listen to what I was saying about AIDS and its sexual transmission, and yet young people who watch soap operas got the impression the only reason you got out of bed in the morning was to jump into somebody else's.

Former U.S. surgeon general C. Everett Koop

A man will give up almost anything except his suffering.

John Cleese

Let's not jeopardize an upstanding citizen's life because too much money was spent trying to save a wounded addict with drugs stashed in his underwear.

Garrett Paul Calhoun

FRY NOW. PAY LATER.

An American Cancer Society poster on the dangers of sunbathing

Living Needs Benefit.

Option made available to the terminally ill or those permanently confined to a nursing home to collect almost all the death benefit from their life insurance policy before they die

Our study indicated that the most intense psychological disturbances [for afflicted women] were associated with the potential of having breast cancer, not with loss or conservation of the breast.

Professor William Wolberg

The number of syphilis cases increased from 27,000 in 1986 to 44,000 in 1989, a 41 year high.

According to federal health officials

Top 10 causes of death:
1. Heart disease
2. Cancers
3. Stroke
4. Accidents
5. Chronic obstructive pulmonary diseases
6. Pneumonia and influenza
7. Diabetes
8. Suicide
9. Chronic liver disease
10. Homicide

According to the National Center for Health Statistics

It wasn't that long ago that one of the major treatments for ulcers was a milk diet. Now milk has been recognized as not being good for ulcer patients.

Professor Donald Kastens

The beer-drinking rats lived nearly six times longer—nine months instead of a month and a half—than their teetotaling counterparts. They also had lower blood cholesterol and fewer enlarged hearts.

According to a study by Leslie Klevay

Our overloaded emergency departments are a manifestation of our inability to deal with drug abuse, homelessness and uncompensated medical care.

David F. Baehren, M.D.

Infectious diseases are not the vestige of our premodern past but the price we pay for living in an organic world.

Stephen S. Morse

In the next century, I believe, surgery will be dominated by transplant technology and remember, the next century will begin in just nine years.

Dr. Thomas Starzl

Today's teens take a minute longer to run a mile than did teens ten years ago. The reason may be . . . too many teens are sitting around watching TV and playing video games.

Karen McNulty, reporting on a study by Chrysler Corporation and the Amateur Athletic Union

Dog bites account for 1% of all emergency room admissions.

According to a report in the JOURNAL OF THE AMERICAN MEDICAL ASSOCIATION

Star-Kist will not purchase any tuna caught in association with dolphins.

H.J. Heinz chairman Anthony O'Reilly

Chapter 6

THE WRITTEN WORD

ON WRITING

When students fall in love with me I want to tell them I'm in the dream that won't last; there are more pleasures in the text.

Poet Stephen Dunn

The speech writers write the draft . . . and the committee here or there works on it and then the President gets it. He takes out the red meat. And then you ask why it doesn't sing.

An anonymous White House aide, describing the presidential speech process

You don't need to know a whole lot of spelling to write a best-seller.

Best-selling author Charles J. Givens

The essential matter of history is not what happened but what people thought or said about it.

Frederic Maitland

The best day is when I can write a lead that will cause a reader at his breakfast table the next morning to spit up his coffee, clutch his heart and shout, "My God! Martha, did you read this?"

Pulitzer prize winning police reporter Edna Buchanan

I did use [alcohol]—often in conjunction with music—as a means to let my brain conceive visions that the unaltered, sober brain has no access to.

Author William Styron

Anticipate, and imitate. You can preclude and disspirit a holocaust by depriving it of originality.

Writer Lorrie Moore in "Like Life"

Anyone who has a choice and doesn't choose *not* to write is a fool . . . the work is hard, the perks are few, the pay is terrible, and the product, when it's finally finished is pure joy.

Novelist Mary Lee Settle

[Translation] is an impossible but necessary process. There is no perfect way to do it, and much of it must be found for each particular poem, as we go.

Poetry translator W. S. Merwin

. . . Confidence is above all what it takes [to write a trilogy], surely. You must be confident that you have staying power, confidence your characters and plot will remain interesting, confidence you can get the pace right, because this is going to go on for a very long time.

Margaret Forster

[The great works of children's literature] mark current assumptions and express the imaginative, unconventional, non-commercial view of the world in its simplest and purest form.

Alison Lurie in DON'T TELL THE GROWN-UPS

The novelist must each time find something that has not been written about before, or at least not in his way; and at the same time, if he is to write about it for three or four hundred pages, he must know it with terrific intimacy. In a novel, the emotion is in the details.

Author Robert Daley

A writer is a kind of spy, an unconscious spy. You use everything that's ever happened to you, and you're never, ever bored.

Author Countess of Romanones

People want to know why I do this, why I write such gross stuff. I like to tell them I have the heart of a small boy—and I keep it in a jar on my desk.

Stephen King

When I write a novel, I get to play all the parts. I play the men, women, and children. I decide who gets hired, who gets fired, and who gets laid.

Kirk Douglas

My thesis advisor in graduate school once told me to write the whole narrative out—even in the crudest form—and *then* revise. My writing immediately improved.

Author John Murray

Writer, if you want to write, write! . . . As readers, we are the ultimate authority. We're up to the task.

Kenneth Logsdon

What is it we really demand of our fiction? . . . A fictional world that differs defiantly from the familiar, a language that opens up to us the hidden resources of our own speech and the self-generating perpetuation of the intriguing.

Writer Richard Martin

The important poems being written now may well be those being written far from the academy, and not intended for publication . . . poems that say things we are not ready to hear.

Edward Foster

ABOUT WRITERS

When Taraborrelli wrote about Diana Ross in his fawning 1985 bio, *Diana*, he called her "my star." She must not have sent the guy a thank-you note. In this book [*Call Her Miss Ross*], an often bitchy bio, Taraborrelli writes like a man scorned.

Reviewer Alan Carter

This is one sequel which I am sure he'd rather not star in.

Newswoman Faith Daniels on the second lawsuit for plagiarism against Eddie Murphy

I don't know how good a writer I am, but I'm a very good interviewer . . . I write "Shut up" in my notebook a lot. Or just "S.U." If you looked through my notebooks, you'd see a lot of S.U's.

Robert Caro

Coleridge is love, spreading outward from the family to society at large, like the ripples on a pine; . . . he is the breath that plays over the strings of the harp of an organic nature; he is the life force, "nature's fast ever-acting energy."

Jonathan Wadsworth reviewing the book
COLERIDGE, by Richard Holmes

The style is clitoral, as far as I'm concerned.

Professor Paula Bennett commenting on
Emily Dickinson's poetry

I suppose my model is nearly always Dostoevsky, a man of very strong convictions, but his characters illustrated and incarnated in the most powerful themes and issues and trends of his day. I think maybe the greatest novel of all times is the *Brothers Karamazov*.

Novelist Walker Percy

On the evidence, however, Tom Clancy's macho novels are not meant so much for men as overgrown boys. The sexiest items in his novels are the pieces of military hardware, which are unfailingly described in loving, sensuous detail.

Novelist Mordecai Richler

America's greatest contribution to pop literature is the tough-guy hero, that hard-punching, hard-drinking, hard-loving macho *mensch* who can't help annoying the bad guys, even while he makes every woman swoon.

Author Bill Kent

Steele's knowlege of Viet Nam seems to have been gleaned from World War II movies.

Ralph Novac in review of the book MESSAGE FROM NAM
by Danielle Steele

I don't make such a distinction as I used to between the two. Now I feel that my fiction and my non-fiction are really saying the same thing.

Author Peter Matthiessen

[Alberto Moravia] is concerned with man's search to find a place for himself in the world, a way of attaching himself to some spar and all the chaos and shipwreck around, to stop himself floating off into nowhere, falling off the edge of the world.

Rosemary Stoyle in a review of JOURNEY TO ROME
by Alberto Muradia

And with history exploding around him, he regrettably chooses to focus his book on himself, producing a shallow "I" witness account of the powerful people he has worked with or met.

Jeff Gillenkirk in a review of IN THE SHADOW OF THE DOME:
CHRONICLES OF A CAPITOL HILL AID *by Mark Bisnow*

Richard Hough is right to say that the marriage [of Winston and Clementine Churchill] worked so well largely because of the couple's simple and much to be admired practice of taking long stints away from one another.

Critic Andrew Roberts

Ann Beattie is a master of interaction. Her stories are propelled not so much by event as by the accumulation of the details that build a life as surely as the tumble and drift of sediment builds shale or sandstone. Pay attention to the small things, she tells us.

T. Coraghessan Boyle in the review of PICTURING WILL
by Ann Beattie

I think the appeal of Alice Walker is that her ideas coincide with this Reaganite attitude that all of the social problems in the United States are caused by black men.

Novelist Ishmael Reed

Unfortunately, Turow seriously undermined whatever literary claims his book *Presumed Innocent* might have had by what I consider an act of malicious bad faith: the revelation near the novel's end of crucial information that the first-person narrator has until then concealed from the reader.

Critic Robert Towers

Most people don't care about authors. It's like being in a Lacrosse Hall of Fame. I call up almost any office and have to spell my name

Author Kurt Vonnegut

BOOKS

Despite its length, *The Kennedys of Massachusetts* is really a "Cliffs Notes" version of history. But although it is simplistic and streamlined, there's no denying it is also quite entertaining.

Critic David Hiltbrand

From Hemingway she takes a setting filled with beautiful, bored rich people and bullfighters; from [Judith] Krantz she takes beautiful, bored rich people and sex. Call this cross-pollination THE SCUM ALSO RISES.

> *Reviewer Leah Rozen on new novel, FANTASIES,*
> *by Beverly Sassoon*

I'M STILL HERE

> *Title of Eartha Kitt's autobiography*

LENT: THE SLOW FAST

> *Title of a collection of short stories by Starkey Flythe*

America's Vietnamese war was the conflict which saw the venerable cliche about "history belonging to the victors" finally laid to rest. The U.S. lost the war, but retained the book and movie rights; the resulting deluge of print and celluloid has meant that the mundane details of the GI experience have become familiar almost to the point of utter banality.

> *Charles Sharr Murray in the review of the novel, CW 2,*
> *by Layne Heath*

As he sees it, the job of the artist is to ignore the obvious, accepted standards of artistic excellence in favor of his own vision. The job of the critics and audience is to resist this vision until the determination of the artist overcomes their resistance.

> *Barbara Howell reviewing the book, SOME FREAKS,*
> *by David Mamet*

Readers are conned into buying trash or into thinking mediocre stuff a masterpiece by methods not wholly unlike the marketing of high-return investment trusts and similar risky ventures.

> *Paul Johnson on the marketing of books*

In the end, selling books as in selling beer or promoting restaurants, the public taste determines whether you succeed or fail.

> *Alan Massie*

I found it a grating, uncomfortable book to read. It was a literary equivalent to that moment when you are so tired that you feel a squirming itch inside your muscles and you cannot get at it to scratch.

Genesist P. Orrindge reviewing MEMOIRS OF A BASTARD
ANGEL: THE AUTOBIOGRAPY OF HAROLD NORSE

If "African American" is to be a point of departure for "Cultural Integrity"rather than an empty symbol to mask the realities of the ongoing deterioration of society, radical, thoroughgoing changes in culture and politics are required. The book . . . that will point the way to these changes and the ways and means to get African Americans to adopt them has not yet been written. It is sorely needed.

Ronald C. Smith

Book sellers say that what finally counts is originality of material and a realistic appreciation of the scope and nature of the potential readership. These are what will make not just a best seller, but a well-published and well-read book.

Editor Gayle Feldman

It is as if El Greco offered to draw you a portrait in under a minute.

Wilfrid Sheed on Anthony Burgess' biography of Hemingway

Asked about his contract—reportedly a four-book, 50 million deal—[Sidney Sheldon] replies, "I don't like talking about money. . . . I'm overpaid. I would write books for nothing."

Diedre Donahue

Vineland isn't another *Gravity's Rainbow*. What would have been the point of writing another *Gravity's Rainbow* when the world already has one of them? In fact, the one thing Pynchon was pretty certain *not* to do was write another *Gravity's Rainbow*.

Brian McHale

There's no doubt that these are narcissistic narratives. But they are narcissistic in the sense of their primary involvement with (non)-identity, and not a secondary, self-sucking narcissism of contemporary consumer-realism classic that merely mirrors the latest in clubs and commodities.

Kurt Hollander in a review of X IN PARIS *by Michael Brodsky*

When his arms went around me, glints of light sparked in my head as if from a knife sharpening on a wheel, and my veins felt filled with warm, carbonated water.

Carolyn Cassady describing sex with author Jack Kerouac in her book OFF THE ROAD

If this makes Jane [Fonda] sound as if she had the habit of squeezing people dry and then throwing them away, it may have been true only of her early bulimia-addled years.

Bill Davidson in his book JANE FONDA: AN INTIMATE BIOGRAPHY

You can't love somebody until you learn about hate.

From TROUBLE THE WATER *by Melvin Dixon*

First impressions cannot be trusted, it tells us, an unexamined impulse can prove treacherous. True character is achieved only after a thorough education of the emotions.

Linda Gray Sexton reviewing THE LADY OF SITUATIONS *by Louis Auchincloss*

The meaning of the title is pornographic, but I'm using it metaphorically.

Carrie Fisher on the title of her second novel SURRENDER THE PINK

JOURNALISM

They say this comes with the territory but . . . it's like a hand from hell that continually reaches up to grab my ankles.

Roseanne Barr on tabloids

Did you see Tom Brokaw standing on top of the Berlin Wall, pacing back and forth? And if you look closely in the background you could see Deborah Norville tossing banana peels.

Johnny Carson

A sampling of the most underreported stories of our time:

The U.S. Contra Drug Connection and Bush's Role in the Iran Arms Deal

Unreported Worldwide Nuclear Accidents

Biological Warfare Research in University Laboratories and Shipments of Laboratory Made Germ Specimens through the U.S. Mail

Open Air Testing of Pentagon Manufactured Germs and Viruses

Toxic Waste Dumping on The Third World and over the Mexican Border

Hunger in Africa and its Exacerbation by Gunrunning Profiteers

Torture Condoned and Instigated by CIA in El Salvador

According to Project Censor

Black reporters are as capable of racism as anyone else.

Civil rights leader Julian Bond

I'm getting terrible press. It's so unfair. I'm really a very nice person. Can you tell me what to do? I'm willing to pay you.

Nancy Reagan as quoted by astrologer Joan Quigley in her book, WHAT DOES JOAN SAY?

But it does something real insidious to you to take those checks. He felt really [awful] about it. All's he did was buy drugs with it and try to kill himself. You feel so horrible and so attacked.

Roseanne Barr on her husband's stint as a stringer for the NATIONAL ENQUIRER

A celebrity death brings enormous competitive pressure to pull out all the stops to get exclusives and dig up the dirt. . . . The deaths of Elvis Presley and Grace Kelly created a whole industry of public interest and big bucks for years after their deaths.

Steve Tinney, former entertainment writer for the NATIONAL ENQUIRER *and the* GLOBE

At one time you have to say, "Am I an American, or am I a journalist?" The fact is, I am an American journalist. The definition of an American journalist is that he tries to be an honest broker of information and tries to report it accurately and fairly, even if he disagrees with your point of view.

Dan Rather

Journalism rapidly is becoming one of the world's most dangerous occupations. . . . More than 40 journalists were killed in 1989, another 90 were assaulted, and over 250 arrested.

Joe Saltzman

American journalists who fashion themselves blank slates get written on by some pretty unsavory characters, that is, used. . . . You just have to be willing to risk some disfavor and misunderstanding if that is the price of covering the subject fairly.

Meg Greenfield

In journalism, legends are not merely born. They are worked at.

Anthony Spaeth

Journalism is different from my parent's day, Alice. We do nothing but follow each other around, pretend that television hasn't scooped us all. We're not tracing truth. We're chasing each other. The only thing that is real is what comes from here. He tapped his head. Creation! Invention!

Craig in the novel THE HONG KONG FOREIGN CORRESPONDENTS CLUB *by Anthony Spaeth*

In their later years, journalists are often prey to a temptation to write their memoirs. Usually, it is one they are wise to resist.

Jay W. M. Thompson

AND SO FORTH

. . . This country is so urbanized we think low-fat milk comes from cows on aerobic-exercise programs.

Writer P. J. O'Rourke

. . . a criminal, a thief, an unclean person, a blackmailer, a psychotic, an extortionist, a forger, a perjurer, a liar, a whore, an arsonist and a squatter.

Tom Clark and Dick Kleiner, authors of ROCK HUDSON, FRIEND OF MINE, *referring to Marc Christian*

Divorced people like to keep tabs on each other; hatred is a very strong tie.

Bernie in the novel, I ANNA, *by Elsa Lewin*

How beneficial it would be if modern politicians were obliged to follow the courtly tradition of dispatching a sonnet instead of massaging the statistics. Imagine the corridors of power inhabited by people who could rhyme, scan, and make sense.

Antonio Nasag

I think the late 20th Century is in many ways a story without a plot. With everything that is familiar collapsing around us, the only way to chart the journey ahead is through the imagination.

Author Jeanette Winterson commenting on her latest novel, SEXING THE CHERRY, *which also has no plot*

The Celts have never had an empire, despite the title of this book. Imperialism requires discipline, self-confidence and respect for authority. These are not Celtic characteristics.

Richard Cavendish in a review of THE CELTIC EMPIRE *by Peter Berresford Ellis*

Longevity Is The Best Revenge.

Title of a review of Richard Nixon's most recent book in
THE NEW YORK TIMES BOOK REVIEW

The events of the 80's—especially the 1989 happenings—
have developed with such dizzing speed that there has been
really no time to absorb them fully . . . but they have proved
beyond any doubt that life pays no attention to academic
predictions, projections, and analyses.

Tad Szulc in his book, THEN AND NOW

History chooses itself, it is not chosen by those present, no
matter how often they ensure they are present.

Genesist P. Orrindge

The figure of the priest is a very potent one for Catholic
women. I think it shapes the way we respond to figures of
male authority . . . the male authority figure was a sacred
personage, as well.

Novelist Mary Gordon

The critical feature of all pornography is not that it deals
with sexual themes, but that it eroticizes violence, humiliation, degradation, and other explicit forms of abuse.

Mary Ellen Ross

New York Times Co. is offering a videocassette that tells
how to cover nuclear events more safely.

According to the WALL STREET JOURNAL

Knowlege is all we really have to share with others; with
that, they can design their lives.

Dominic Anthony Perreira

Liquor, once you're hooked on it, is a hard habit to break.
Like God.

Novelist Mordecai Richler

"America is back standing tall," said the President, after a Marine amphibious unit of 1,250 heavily armed men and two Ranger battalions defeated 636 Cuban construction workers and 43 soldiers. . . . By March the Associated Press had figured out that more medals had been issued by the Army than the number of soldiers wounded in the assault.

Richard J. Barnet commenting on the 1983 Grenada invasion in his book, THE ROCKETS RED GLARE

Saturday night movies in the Gym were the social climax of the week. Everyone put on the Big Dog. The hucklebuckin hambones Afropicked and jerrycurled their cornrows . . . the vatos and street bravos wrapped their cleanest bandannas around Dippity-Doed razorcuts . . . the white boys splashed on fifi water . . . the Q Wing punks and B CAT queens greased on party paint and shimmied into tightass state blues.

First novelist Seth Morgan describing Saturday night in prison in HOMEBOY

A great speech from the leader to the people eases our isolation, breaks down the walls, includes people: It take's them inside a spinning thing and makes them part of the gravity.

Peggy Noonan

He gratefully matched her ersatz rhythms, gripped her like a boogie board, and rode her wavelets till they became breakers, body-surfing in on them until they crashed to shore.

From the novel, EXES, *by Dan Greenburg*

We live in a highly acquisitive society that has taught us to believe that possessions bring happiness. . . . Through my own battle with shopping and spending I found a slew of other activities that have brought me far *greater* pleasure.

From WOMEN WHO SHOP TOO MUCH *by Carolyn Wesson*

"The Grate Society"
> *Subtitle for an article on the homeless in*
> WASHINGTON MONTHLY

What's black and white and brown and looks good on a lawyer?
A doberman.
> *Novelist Mordecai Richler*

You can hear the page turning in his life.
> *Baxter Black*

His lips split by fever, taste like nickels. His bones are of ice and the ice is wrapped with layers of hot flesh. His head is filled with fluid that exerts pressure at the base of his nose, and his eyes are dry as paper.
> *From* PNEUMONIA, *a short story by Larry Woiwode*

I am hurt but I am not slain! I will lie me down and bleed awhile—then I'll rise and fight again.
> *Quotation from St.Barton's Ode that Richard Nixon, in his book* IN THE ARENA, *claims sustained him during the early days of Watergate*

You are borrowed by everything you love.
> *Poet Bohdan Boychuk*

Chapter 7

SPORTS

THE GAME

Baseball is a tougher sport to master. The football people may argue with me, but it's all strength and power in that game. Baseball is a little more instincts and finesse, coordination.

Kansas City Royals manager John Wathan

The difference between hitting .300 and .270 is a hit and a half a week.

Chicago Cub Mark Grace

The turning point of the game was the coin toss.

John Madden, commenting on the Superbowl

That is what this game is all about. If you can't play this game on emotion don't show up.

Football coach Mike Ditka

The Superbowl is our great national campfire around which we cluster.

George Will

Threepeat.

Superbowl 49ers, on future aspirations

We have to score more points. That's the bottom line.

Kansas City Chiefs quarterback Steve DeBerg

If it were up to me, I'd love to go back to one-platoon football right now. It would get us back to a lot of basic values.

Penn State coach Joe Paterno

[Today's football players] couldn't do it. They'd run out of gas. Before the half, they'd be suckin' and huffin' and puffin'. . . . One platoon football would let us really find out how great they are.

Former linebacker Chuck Bednarik

The 1990 Goodwill Games will not reduce the nuclear arms stockpile, cut pollution, or reduce overpopulation. Nevertheless, on July 20, when 2,500 top athletes march into Seattle, they bring the world a little closer together, and we all will take another small step toward survival and peaceful coexistence.

Ted Turner

The best golf course in the world: Pebble Beach
The best ballpark for baseball fans: Fenway Park
The best football factory in the nation: Penn State
The best place to see a hockey game: Chicago Stadium
The best college football state: California

According to SPORT

If the United States wants to take over the world, it should do the dirty deed on World Cup Finals day. There'll be no opposition. The rest of the world, *all* of it, will be far too busy following the antics of 22 soccer players to worry about minor things such as takeovers, invasions or coups.

Paul Gardner

It is a terrible thing to cheer people when they beat each other. Maybe it is a deep instinct.

Bo Derek, commenting on the
Sugar Ray Leonard-Roberto Duran fight

Without a doubt, he won the bout.

Banner on the boxing match between Tyson and his opponent
James Buster Douglas

Americans have always liked to believe that their national pastime exemplifies the ideals of free competition, fair play, sportsmanship and the quest for excellence. It is something of a paradox, that professional baseball has been operated since its inception by men who, more often than not, have demonstrated a proclivity for greed, avarice, coersion, or collusion.

Richard Regen in a review of the book, THE MINORS,
by Neil J. Sullivan

People wonder why the same guys aren't out there day in and day out, especially after they've been effective for a couple of days in a row. Basically you can't afford to abuse these people. . . . It's a difficult situation when the game is on the line to know you can't put in the guy who everybody knows should be there. You take a short-term gain and the long-term loss every time.

California Angels manager Doug Rader

Swimming one mile is like running four miles in terms of energy expenditure.

HEALTHACTION MANAGERS

The fourteenth World Cup was a disappointment. . . . In times past, the better team won: Nowadays, it is the team that fearfully avoids making mistakes.

Ludger Schulze

For the fans, soccer is more than a sport: It is the best indicator of "National Virtues" and each confrontation, a paroxysmal experience, is a ritualized war.

LE MONDE DIPLOMATIQUE

At least as far as soccer is concerned, for the time being, America is a Third World country.

Silvio Garioni

If you can somehow put the fear of God into the whole team [by fighting], that's a pretty good advantage.

Hockey general manager Harry Sinden

Basketball is the most popular, but the fastest growing sports of interest to women are soccer and cross-country.

According to Professors R. Vivian Acosta and
Linda Jean Carpenter

Horses are like strawberries; you must enjoy them while you can, because they don't last long.

Trainer Charlie Whittingham

The losing football team gets more reinforcement than kids with perfect ACT scores.

Professor Michael Shaughnessy

THE BUSINESS OF SPORTS

Major League baseball is a closed confederation of 26 business persons or corporations who have been awarded a monopoly by Congress. They are free to run their exclusive enterprise without the usual restraints of the nation's antitrust laws. Under the guise of operating a public trust, they receive unique tax benefits and take in millions of dollars each year.

Havelock Hews and Neil Cohen

All I know is that on airplane trips, David's wallet will be considered carry-on baggage.

Pat Williams, Orlando Magic General Manager, on N.B.A.
Commissioner David Stern's new five year,
$27.5 million contract

[I'd] like the games speeded up. It seems like we play 3 hour games everyday. I blame it on television coverage of the games.

LA Dodger Mickey Hatcher, Jr.

They wanted an arm and a leg.
Martina Navratilova explaining why she never insured her
left arm with Lloyds of London

Swimsuit issue? If you really wanted to show swimsuits, you could have laid them on the table or dressed a mannequin. Give me a break.

Sharon Hogan

I wish to express my gratitude to the feminists who protested your swimsuit issue at the main newstand in Harvard Square. It drew my attention to your magnificent magazine celebrating the wonders of the female body.

Charles G. Thomas

I won't be able to read your magazine anymore. After seeing the cover of the swimsuit issue, my wife forbade me from buying another issue.

Andy Buren

On any given weekend during the NFL season, some 40 million people wager $3-4 billion on men wearing pads and helmets.

Danny Sheridan

Unlike male athletes, who usually are pictured demonstrating raw power, women featured in the media most often are shown in passive, non-action settings such as lounging by a pool, caressing their sports equipment, or smiling pleasantly in a dress and high heels.

According to Professor Mary Jo Kane

You start to feel like a pimp.
Coach Bo Schembechler, University of Michigan, on recruiting

Recruiting is like shaving. If you don't do it everyday, you look like a bum.

Recruiter David Kaplan

Sports grossed more than $63 billion in 1988, making it the country's 22nd largest industry.

According to SPORTING NEWS

We deserve every penny we're getting. We are entertainers. People watch us, just like they go to the movies. If *anybody* could be doing what we're doing, then we're overpaid. . . . There are only 28 starting [NFL] quarterbacks in the world. It's a unique, specific group.

Green Bay Packer quarterback Don Majkowski

Reggie [Jackson] has advice for investors. Gather future Hall-of-Famers, *now*. And that includes Reggie Jackson. Mr. October has about 2,000 of his own cards, including 100 of his rare rookie card.

SPORT

There are three things money can't buy—love, happiness, and an American League Pennant.

The late Edward Bennett Williams

It's a sports junkie's dream. . . . It's called interactive television, and the technology puts the fan in the broadcast booth, letting you choose the way you want to see the game. . . . By using a special remote control and cable box, you'll have a choice of what part of the game you want to watch from a variety of camera angles.

Matt Edelson

Arnold Palmer at 60 can't putt for the big drawer purses that he won in his prime, but he drives to the bank with $9 million every year in fees from Hertz, Paine-Webber, Sears, Pennzoil, Lanier, and Cadillac, and more than 70 licenses worldwide.

Timothy Carlson

Hockey great Wayne Gretzky [annual salary $3.2 million] takes home more than $4 million from: Nike ($600,000), Coca Cola ($900,000), American Express ($100,000), General

Mills ($300,000), Zurich Insurance ($300,000) and various products he licenses ($2.5 million).

Timothy Carlson

The New York Yankee's Don Mattingly became baseball's highest paid player Monday, when he signed a five year contract extension worth $19.3 million.

Tom Pedulla of Gannet News Service

The National Football League's licensing division . . . is planning a line of souvenir items for the pets of America. Doggy sweaters, kitty litter boxes, even a $200 doghouse in the shape of a football helmet . . . .

Sports columnist Gary Peterson

Football is still No. 1 for me. It's got to be No. 1. It's making me more money.

Defensive back Deion Sanders

"NACEX"—(National Collectors Exchange) a new electronic system for buying, selling and trading baseball cards.

*Developed by the Major League Baseball Players
Alumni Association*

THE PLAYERS

01832061.

Pete Rose's prison I.D. number

But I signed a contract, and I pitch for what I signed for. Think about it—your signature on a contract is the same as your word.

Nolan Ryan, on how he ended up with a pay cut

Top 10 sport incomes:
  1. Sugar Ray Leonard, WBC super middle weight champ, $27,450,000
  2. Mike Tyson, heavyweight, $11,200,000

3. Roberto Duran, super middleweight, $7,572,000
4. Thomas Hearns, super middleweight, $6,600,000
5. Patrick Ewing, center, New York Knicks, $3,575,000
6. Robin Yount, outfielder, Milwaukee Brewers, $3,200,000
7. Wayne Gretzsky, center, LA Kings, $2,720,000
8. Kirby Puckett, outfield, Minnesota Twins, $2,709,000
9. Charles Barkly, forward, Philadelphia 76ers, $2,600,000
10. Roger Clemens, pitcher, Boston Red Sox, $2,600,000

According to SPORT

"1000 a day" and "3000 a day"

The number of pushups and situps, respectively,
Herschel Walker says he does

Some kids want to join the circus when they grow up. Others want to be big-league baseball players. I feel lucky. When I came to the Yankee's I got to do both.

Craig Nettles

The older great athletes are mentally tough. They can push themselves longer and harder. They can read the signs and characteristics of other players, and know their sport to the nth degree.

David Barlow, co-director of the Sports Science Center

The young go all on their genetics, but guys like Carlton [Fisk] are different. Right after the game, they're back in the weight room. It's a difference of attitudes. They understand that as long as you train, you can stay with the game.

Trainer Phil Claussen

He has remarkable athletic ability. He scrambles like no quarterback in the game ever has. You gotta force this guy into the pocket because he'll run, cut, reverse his field, cut, run, then all of a sudden throw deep. No one makes things happen like Randall Cunningham.

LA Rams linebacker Kevin Greene

Randall Cunningham. Without a doubt [the toughest quarterback]. The guy can do so many things; he can beat you so many ways. You're not really gonna shut him down; you just contain him. And that's just tough, trying to contain him. He can roll out and throw it 60, 70 yards.

Cleveland Browns defensive tackle Michael Dean Perry

Bo [Jackson] is truly an American hero; not only is he an excellent athlete, but he is an individualist. Bo takes charge of what he does, and he gets the job done without taking crap from anybody else.

Amy Gunther

He stands for truth, justice and the Hulkamania way.

Wrestler Hulk Hogan speaking about another wrestler

The competition and the strategy of football, I like a lot, but, again, I always said I'd never play it over 5 years, professionally, and now it's been seven. Frankly, I didn't think I liked it enough to stay this long.

Herschel Walker

At one time Ken Stabler was considered the NFL's most accurate passer. He was hitting 50% of his throws when most of the league was in the 40's. Now the league is approaching 60% and [Joe] Montana's at 70%.

Bronco Defensive Coordinator Ade Phillips

I like to make history.

Boxer James Buster Douglas

Only my best

Motto worn on the hat of James Buster Douglas

Most experts think I'm a fluke, and that's good. It inspires me *and* makes opponents think they can whup me easy. . . . Short Man [Tyson] hasn't treated me fair. Next time I'll fold him like a card table.

Buster Douglas

When I was champ, the trainers told me what to do, and I just did it. They put ingredients in during training, but I did not know the recipe. Sometimes, I came out a German chocolate cake. Now, I'm the cook, and I always come out like prime ribs.

Former heavyweight champ George Foreman

Mike Tyson's soft around the chin. As soon as things don't work profitably for him, he quits. . . . Man, his day is over. The kids even know that. All of them Mike Tyson Nintendo games are on the bottom of everybody's toy box now.

George Foreman

Somebody who's a good mother or a good father, a good teacher—they're more important than professional athletes.

Detroit Red Wings Steve Yzerman

I'm telling you right now, within two years, Will Clark's contract [$15 million over four years] is going to look like a great bargain.

Al Rosen

Will [Clark] firmly believes he is better than the pitcher. He won't take the attitude that he's going to let the pitcher defeat him. I don't think I have as strong a will as he does yet. I still have times when I'm overmatched.

Chicago Cubs Mark Grace

Jose Canseco wasn't the first ballplayer with a 900 number for fans, only the first to be criticized for it.

SPORT

The best male physiques of the 1980s decade:
    Greg Louganis
    Sylvester Stallone
    Arnold Schwarzenegger
    Bo Jackson
    Michael Jordan

The best female physiques in the 1980s decade:
Jane Fonda
Jackie Joyner-Kersee
Madonna
Raquel Welch
Steffi Graf
  According to the International Federation of Bodybuilders

Can't you let a guy sulk in peace.
  Quarterback John Elway to journalists a couple of hours
  after his Superbowl loss

Every head must bow, every knee must bend, every tongue
must confess that Ali was the greatest. . . . But Mike Tyson
will prove a worthy successor to that legacy.
  Boxing promoter Don King

The Center Is Holding.
  Headline over a story about basketball center Patrick Ewing
  in THE NATIONAL—the first all sports daily newspaper
  distributed nationwide

When I go on a field, I know I'm good, and I can make
anything happen. It's just my personality. When I'm out
there, I'm very, very confident.
  Green Bay Packer quarterback Don Majkowski

[Jose Canseco's] an awesome physical specimen. I'm big,
but not nearly as big as him. My homers just make it over
by 10 feet, where his make it over by 100 feet.
  Mark McGwire

There's no human on earth like Canseco. He's the most
devastating offensive machine I've ever seen.
  Count Parker

The best pure athlete in team sports: Bo Jackson
The best player in baseball: Jose Canseco
The best all-around game in women's tennis: Steffi Graf

The best all-around game in men's tennis: Stefan Edberg
The best quarterback in the NFL: Joe Montana
The best player in the NFL: Reggie White
The best boxer in the world: Julio Cesar Chavez (Mexico)
The best hockey player in the world: Wayne Gretzky
The best player in the NBA: Michael Jordan

According to SPORT

I think we're going to redefine what 40-year-olds can do.
*1972 Olympic Gold Medal Swimmer, Mark Spitz, on his
efforts to make the 1992 Olympic swimming team*

On the football field he is larger than life. He does everything right. He made me sick when I was playing against
him. I'd say, "Okay Joe, screw something up already."

Matt Millen on quarterback Joe Montana

In the last ten years three star quarterbacks all white had
tested positive for cocaine but received no mandatory counseling or treatment. In addition the NFL had a hit list of
black players whom the league wanted to catch through
testing.

As reported on WJAL, in Washington, D.C.

Q: What can you do to improve?
Bronco owner Pat Bowlen: Send in an assassin after
Montana.

Comment made apparently during the Superbowl

[Nolan] Ryan is the best pitcher ever by one crucial standard: people don't hit what he throws.

Richard Corliss

If you see a defense team with dirt and mud on their backs
they've had a bad day.

Former football coach John Madden

Many studies have shown that athletes generally have better
mental health than others, but overtraining can eliminate

that advantage. Once an athlete becomes stale, the only known remedy is rest, which is usually the last thing a competitive athlete wants to do.

Professor Kathleen Ellickson

Before she could ask the first question, Morris said: "I don't talk to people when I'm naked, especially women, unless they are on top of me or I'm on top of them."

DETROIT FREE PRESS publisher Neil Shine

AND SO FORTH

The divorce rate in cities with major league baseball teams is 23% lower than the rate in cities now seeking big league franchises, among them Buffalo, Denver, Indianapolis, Miami and Phoenix.

According to psychologist Howard Markman

Perhaps coach Tom Landry's spiritual life was "founded upon a rock" (Matthew 7:25) but his "business," as he called the Cowboys, was built on prairie dust. On Texas-sized egos. On greed. Excess. Sex appeal. Adultery. Lies. Oil. Alcohol. Arrogance. Gusher luck. On a towering media-made facade known as Cowboys mystique.

From GOD'S COACH: THE HYMNS, HYPE AND HYPOCRISY OF TOM LANDRY'S COWBOYS, by Skip Bayless

A new FBI test can detect cocaine use by analyzing hair. Once the drug is deposited in a person's hair shaft, it remains there permanently.

According to SELF

If you ain't got a hernia yet you ain't pulling your share of the load.

A sign on the wall of George Steinbrenner's office

Winning means everything. You show me a good loser and I'll show you a loser.

George Steinbrenner

This is a very sophisticated club. . . . All the greens break toward the hot tub.

Snoopy in AN EDUCATED SLICE, *by Charles M. Schulz*

The environment is modest, and [Deion Sanders'] living here with his fiancee, Carolyn Chambers, their daughter Diondra, and a couple of friends.

Journalist Bill Chastain

After devouring a tackle, a guard and a quarterback, what do you wash them down with? . . . Gatorade.

Ad for Gatorade

Sports magazines with the highest paid circulation:
1. *Sports Illustrated*
2. *Street & Smith's*
3. *Golf Digest*
4. *The American Hunter*
5. *Golf Magazine*

According to USA TODAY

This year 25 sons of former major leaguers have played in the majors.

According to SPORT

Prices charged by top athletes for their signature at the All-American Baseball Card Convention:
1. Kareem Abdul-Jabbar—$24
2. Jose Canseco—$22
3. Willie Mays—$20
4. Rickey Henderson—$19
5. Joe Morgan—$9
   Gordie Howe—$9
   Bart Starr—$9
6. Don Larsen—$5

According to USA TODAY

VakuTak
> *A heat-vacuum molding process that reshapes boots around player's feet while he's wearing them*

Ebonite Thunderbolt
> *A new bowling ball, designed by Carmen Salvino, which more accurately redistributes the weight lost when fingerholes are drilled*

Auto racing is the fastest growing spectator sport in America. Forty-one million Americans watched at least one race on television and 28 million went to a race.

> *According to Nordhaus Research*

Even if you lose a couple, so what? Babe Ruth struck out 1330 times, the people remember the 714 home runs.

> *Anonymous*

The top sports for injuries in high school:
1. Football
2. Wrestling
3. Softball
4. Gymnastics

> *Kathleen Hart*

Chapter 8

ENTERTAINMENT

TELEVISION

The best things in life are someone else's.

From "Married . . . With Children"

Despite the pseudo-lower-middle-class realism of "Rose-anne" and "Married . . . with Children," the implicit message in much of prime time remains almost effortless economic entitlement. . . . TV characters are never rooted in Toledo or Omaha; instead, most spring to life magically equipped with sprawling houses and apartments in glamorous cities like New York and Los Angeles.

Critic Walter Shapiro

Ah, home sweet hell

Al Bundy of "Married . . . With Children"

It's difficult to get a female perspective on the show ["Saturday Night Live"]. It's always been a frat show, as far as I'm concerned. The women have always been overtalented and underused.

Nora Dunn about her departure from "Saturday Night Live"

The President and Mrs. Bush's favorite T.V. programs: "60 Minutes," "America's Funniest Home Videos," "Murder, She Wrote."

According to First Lady Barbara Bush

What (ABC) gets in the end is a happy, well-adjusted woman who can live with herself, who can open up that show with a smile on her face. They get a person sitting on that set that men and women are going to relate to. Much more so than some little ambitious single gal. I've said, "You know something? What you're buying in me is a mother image."

Joan Lunden, reflecting on motherhood and her tenth anniversary with "Good Morning, America"

You look like you've been reincarnated as a rag.

Roseanne

When I first heard the note of finality in the title of this, the third Hulk revival ["The Death of the Incredible Hulk"], I thought it meant poor David Banner . . . had finally stumbled across a stress-management course.

Critic David Hiltbrand

I've had all I can take of apologists for the entertainment industry telling me it's my responsibility to keep objectionable material away from my teenage children. The TV companies and recording studios must be laughing all the way to the bank while they lay this guilt trip on parents.

Jacqueline Frey

If you are going to break a commandment, you might as well get a little mileage out of it.

Fred Savage on "The Wonder Years"

Parents worry about events they have little control over, such as homicide—but they are less concerned about things like a child's choice of TV programs, which they can influence.

Dr. Gunnard Stickler

Here's a perfect example of what not to do in a high school yearbook, pose with your baby.

Peggy on "Married . . . With Children"

I realized the power TV had over me when:
"We began eating the evening meal in front of the television six nights out of seven."
"I started to use British slang."
"When I taped 'Wheel of Fortune' to view at my leisure."
"I didn't want to look at something my children had made because I would have to stop watching TV."
"My set broke and I wondered what I would do the rest of the night."

From a survey conducted by U.S. CATHOLIC

They're all mine. . . . Of course, I'd trade any one of them for a dishwasher.

Roseanne on "Roseanne," talking about her kids

We had to shoot [the kissing scene] 25 different ways. . . . I was supposed to be freaked out, and I was—so it worked.

"21 Jump Street's" Holly Robinson, on playing a lesbian love scene

She got a suspended sentence. . . . They hanged her.

Rose Nyland on "The Golden Girls"

When I turn my hearing aid up to 10, I can hear a canary breaking wind in Fort Lauderdale.

Sophia on "The Golden Girls"

Who killed Laura Palmer?

"Twin Peaks"

Bart Simpson killed Laura Palmer.

From a cartoon by Rand Carlson

The point is not who killed Laura Palmer. The murder was just to get the ball rolling.

Actress Cheryl Lee of "Twin Peaks"

God did not create this package to work.

Kelly from the TV program "Married . . . With Children"
talking about her body

Remember when you used to watch TV in the 60s and you'd see Perry Como in a cashmere sweater? That's what rock & roll is becoming. It's your parents' music.

Neil Young

THE SIMPSONS

The answers to life's problems are not at the bottom of a bottle. . . . They're on TV.

Homer Simpson of "The Simpsons"

First I lock myself in the laundry room. Then I put the clothes in the washer, watch them go "round and round and round," and get lost in the wonder of it all.

Marge Simpson of "The Simpsons"

Nobody better lay a finger on my Butterfinger

Bart Simpson in an ad for Butterfinger candy

Eat my shorts, man.
I'm Bart Simpson.
Who the hell are you?
Underachiever. And proud of it.

Bart Simpson T-shirts

"The Simpsons" is satire. . . . This program admits that most parents aren't perfect. They haven't worked out their own childhood confusion, and they don't have the answers to all their children's problems.

Victoria A. Rebeck

"The Simpsons" are sort of the anti-Brady's. They invert every convention of what we expect a TV family to be. They are family as post-nuclear mutants—bug-eyed, malevolent, TV-addled, yet somehow sympathetic and, truth be told, a lot more like us than the Cleavers ever were.

TV columnist Jean Marbella

"The Simpsons" are a typical American family. . . . the Simpson children wrestle with problems like peer pressure and their lack of self-understanding while getting sincere but useless—perhaps even damaging—advice from their parents.

Victoria A. Rebeck

["The Simpsons"] represent the American family in all its horror.

Matt Groening, the creator of "The Simpsons"

"The Simpsons" are ordinary, middle-class people—a standard nuclear family—struggling to be normal, and failing miserably because they can't deal with such things as anger and self-pity. They are people who love each other but also happen to drive each other crazy. Humor comes out of the exasperations in the way that normal day-to-day living goes awry for the nutty bunch.

Matt Groening

MUSIC

[Kelly Willis' voice] builds like a windblown fire, leapfrogging octaves and shimmering like an untended garden hose through a lush lawn of heartfelt sentiments.

From the publicity for singer Kelly Willis' album
"Well Travelled Love"

The oboe: an ill wind that nobody blows any good.

Anonymous

Rock & roll is a bit like Las Vegas; guys dressed up in their sisters' clothes pretending to be rebellious and angry but not really angry about anything.

Rock singer Sting

One thing I've noticed that you really can't shock an audience any more. When I started in 1970, it was before movies like *Friday the 13th* and *Nightmare on Elm Street*, and the new generation of horror characters wasn't around yet.

Rocker Alice Cooper

We go to sleep and we wake up to country music. I want that known. But we also do love to hear classical music. And we have it bellowing through the house.

First Lady Barbara Bush

Country music is now the most popular radio format in the U.S.

Blayne Cutler

The fire at midnight burns out by daybreak.

From a country music song

Bobbie Brown's Cuisinart-like hips move in ways no other man's can. He thrusts his pelvis like Elvis, but at 78 r.p.m. His steps are more straight than Michael Jackson's, more fluid than Prince's. And nobody dances dirtier or bumps and grinds more ferociously than Bobby Brown, especially when he gets down on the floor and starts humping.

Journalist Scott Cohen

If they ever want to put on a sticker for people who'd be offended, it should just say "F— you, don't buy this."

Mark Ross

Since every record released surely contains something offensive to someone, sticker them all. Make this as meaningless as the bar code.

Michael Stipe

Women tend to prefer softer music than men. "Hard rock" stations have predominantly male audiences, while "Lite FM" attracts women.

According to a study quoted by AMERICAN DEMOGRAPHICS

Now you're not the only one in
   the world that has problems.
Keep your head straight and
   you can surely solve them.

From "Do the Right Thing" by Redhead

My feeling about things is most music is bad, most films are bad, most TV is bad, most people are bad, but hopefully you can find a little good in anything.

Iggy Pop, CRY-BABY *costar*

I didn't get up for a long time. I didn't shave for a long time. I drank a little.

*Paul McCartney talking about how he felt when
the Beatles broke up*

Five guys on the stage sounding like World War III.

Guitarist Les Paul describing heavy metal music

There's no message to heavy metal. . . . It's about being rich and famous and getting laid.

Penelope Spheeris, director of a documentary on the music

The world doesn't need any more hip. The world doesn't need more cool, more clever. . . . The world needs Picassos, more Mozarts . . . not more Milli Vanillis. Not more haircuts.

Rocker Billy Joel in ROLLING STONE

When you dance with my man, girl, you're stepping on my toes.

From the song "Stop Watching Your Enemies"

Hindsight is heartbreak's best tool.

From the song "My Anniversary for Being a Fool"

The good old days are good and gone now
That's why they're good, because they're gone.

From the song "Old Friend" sung by Marti Jones

Everything I do is a silent I love you. I'm just no good at love out loud.

Country music song

MOVIES

I play a very special groupie. Everybody in the movie sleeps with Jim Morrison. I manage to sleep with him with all my clothes on.

Actress Jennifer Tilly, about her role in Oliver Stone's
THE DOORS

Camille Claudel . . . with his long scenes of frantic plaster-whacking, is about as exciting as watching paint dry.

Critic Clay Warnick

We both screw people for money.

Businessman Edward Lewis (Richard Gere) to hooker Vivian
(Julia Roberts) in the movie PRETTY WOMAN

So does this movie.

Critic Richard Corliss

It was an illusion . . . totally an illusion. We did it with mirrors and light tricks.

Actor Richard Gere, on an earlier appearance
showing frontal nudity

If you get too close to people, you catch their dreams.

From the movie TUCKER

I'm wearing black underwear.

Breathless Mahoney to Dick Tracy when he asks her if she is
grieving for her rubbed-out boyfriend,
in the movie DICK TRACY

Mean green fighting machines on the half shell.

> *Critic Bob Mondello describing the Teenage Mutant*
> *Ninja Turtles*

Movies seen by the President and Mrs. Bush at The White House:

Glory, Driving Miss Daisy, My Left Foot, Pretty Woman, The Fabulous Baker Boys, Naked Gun, Henry the V, Hunt for Red October, Stella.

> *According to Mrs. Bush and the White House Press Office*

If anybody figures that out, call me.

> *President George Bush after seeing the movie*
> FIELD OF DREAMS

About the only thing harder than lambada these days is the fever with which filmmakers are trying to cash in on the bump-and-grind dance.

> *Anita Snow for Associated Press*

It's a woman's movie. The men in it are a reference point.

> *Carrie Fisher on her movie* POSTCARDS FROM THE EDGE

Mutant on the Bounty

> *Title of a horror flick on video tape*

[People] were going out on the streets dropping acid, having love-ins, taking drugs, smoking grass, having sex in the park, having free-speech movements, but they weren't going to the movie theaters, because there was nothing in movie theaters that related to their lives. . . . *Easy Rider* was something they could look at and identify with, and suddenly there were lines around the theaters and suddenly films started changing.

> *Actor Dennis Hopper on the impact of* EASY RIDER

Feminists have always left me alone . . . simply because my films always protray the woman as a superior being.

> *Porn movie king Russ Meyer*

Most of our films have a general good message, sort of the Buddhist belief that good guys will be rewarded and bad guys will be punished. So everybody should be a good guy.

Raymond Chow, producer of TEENAGE MUTANT NINJA TURTLES

I love the [Ninja] Turtles, because they're good and they fight crime.

Three-year-old Max Salvati

The Big Thrill, Family Thighs, Miami Spice, Robo Fox.

Titles of recent skin flicks

We were disappointed about the Academy, but you know, they're old.

Director Spike Lee, on not getting Oscar nominations from the Academy of Motion Picture Arts & Sciences for his highly-touted picture DO THE RIGHT THING

War of the Roses, the nastiest bit of comedy since *Prizzi's Honor*, sends the perfect marriage straight to hell where so many of them go.

Movie critic Jack Matthews

As they acted out their anger and struggled for control, Oliver and Barbara Rose chose their home as the symbolic trophy. In the ensuing battle they destroyed what they were fighting for. Imagine the destruction that takes place when the divorcing couple decides to make their children the prize.

Judge Ronald L. Solove, on the movie WAR OF THE ROSES

When I saw this film, I cried, and then I got angry for all the lost potential, the unfinished lives . . . . It took courage to make this film. It takes courage to watch it, but when you watch it, I promise it will forever change the way you feel about people with AIDS.

Elizabeth Taylor on the documentary COMMON THREADS: STORIES FROM THE QUILT

I think the nightly news is much more violent than anything
I've seen in the movies.

Bruce Waller

Rambo is a pussy.

Sly Stallone as the character Tango, in the movie
TANGO & CASH

Lisa is a piece of pre-digestive pathology. It's a psycho-dash
thriller about a 14-year-old girl who carried on an anonymous phone flirtation with a crazed serial sex killer, a ma-
niac who eventually gets her address and tries to murder
her mother.

Critic Michael Williangton

Lenin said that people vote with their feet. Well, that's
what's happening. They either go, or they don't go. It's all
politics. It's all demographics.

Warren Beatty on movie box office success

While the Motion Picture Association of America [MPAA]
throws a fit over passionate lovemaking scenes, it is sup-
plying R ratings to *Total Recall*, a hymn to extreme and
nonstop violence, and *RoboCop II*, with a scene of a brain
being smashed on the pavement.

Movie critic Roger Ebert

Unless they can put steel condoms on the cyborgs, you'll
see many future RoboCops being born.

Nancy Allen, costar of ROBOCOP II, on the possibility
of more sequels

Bereft of any new ideas, the movie is just an anthology of
jolts to the nervous system. . . . There's really nothing in
the movie than violence, and its dumb violence.

Critic Jack Kroll on the movie ANOTHER 48 HOURS

Broadway is a mess. There is no question about it.

Composer Andrew Lloyd Webber

Another 48 Hours is a movie mainly about the several pretty ways that glass shatters when bullets or bodies are propelled through it.

Critic Richard Schickel

Blaze was a very modern woman way ahead of her time. . . . I think feminists aren't far beyond what Blaze Starr was all about. Today, in movies, they exploit people like me. They make the money. In those days she was making the money. She created herself.

Actress Lolita Davidovich

If people have nothing else to do, they could go see this film. But I wouldn't let it get in the way of the Home Shopping Network.

Bill Murray on his new movie, QUICK CHANGE

Ghosts was about living your life for the moment, because that's all you've got.

Patrick Swayze

Phantom of the Mall: Eric's Revenge. A shopping center where customers get more than they bargained for.

Advertisement for a new horror movie on video tape

ENTERTAINERS ON ENTERTAINING

Some people go to Alcoholics Anonymous, some go to Overeaters Anonymous, I go back to "Santa Barbara." We all have our illnesses.

Soap star Louise Sorel, on being hired for the third time

Once an actress, always a waitress.

Actress Colleen Dewhurst

Good bad taste is always fueled by rage and anger with humor thrown in. Bad bad taste is fueled by stupidity and ignorance, and it comes out as anger.

Filmmaker John Waters

There are certain people that aren't used to being told what to do by a 6'4", 220-lb black man who is a director. I'm supposed to be either robbing their car or opening their door.

TV actor and director Bill Duke

Acting is like lying. The art of lying well. I'm paid to tell elaborate lies.

Actor Mel Gibson

I do not enjoy, for instance, a prostate examination. It's very, very, ah. . . . The whole idea of it offends me, and I always felt. . . . There was something unjust about it. One time my doctor said, "Look, do you think I like it?"

Actor-director Warren Beatty, to a PREMIERE *magazine writer who complained that Beatty was difficult to interview*

People only want to remember me for the one shower in *Psycho*. . . . If I'd known 30 years ago that film students would be going over my body, frame by frame with a microscope, I probably would have asked for a body double.

Actress Janet Leigh

The blood in the shower scene in the movie, *Psycho*, was chocolate syrup.

According to Stephen Rebello in his book ALFRED HITCHCOCK
AND THE MAKING OF PSYCHO

Playing Blanche changed my life more than anything. It helped raise my self-esteem, because Blanche is convinced that she is terrific. And no matter what happens to her, she always bounces back.

Actress Rue McClanahan

[Rue McClanahan] did not get this part [of Blanche Devereau] because [I] believed in her. She got the part by convincing [me] that she was better then I would have ever believed.

"The Golden Girls" executive producer Len Hill

As the embodiment of male sexual infantilism, the Diceman [Andrew Dice Clay] is the mouth of the moment.

Critic Jack Kroll

Walking a tightrope between exploitation and sensible balance is the most difficult job a programmer or host has. To righteously or justifiably tell a whole panoply of experience without overemphasis on teen prostitutes and transsexual lesbians is not easy.

Geraldo Rivera

There is no way you can get people to believe you on screen if they know who you really are through television.

Jack Nicholson

I won't tell you how much money I have, and I won't tell you how much I weigh.

Raymond Burr's ground rules for interviewers

There is an undercurrent of violence in this new obscenity. It will shatter the hopes and dreams of many who hoped and prayed and worked for brotherhood and racial tolerance.

Country singer Johnny Cash on comic Andrew Dice Clay

I was on my way to becoming a serious and credible actor when I chose to do this one job ["The Partridge Family"], a pilot, and then I became this one thing—David Cassidy, the thing.

40-year-old David Cassidy

ON OR ABOUT ENTERTAINERS

Call the police. They always know where I am.

Ike Turner

You know that saying, "An actress is a little bit more than a woman; an actor is a little bit less than a man?" Well, that's except if it's Harrison Ford. He's this incredibly attractive male animal, in every sense of the word.

Actress Carrie Fisher, describing her STAR WARS *co-star for*
VANITY FAIR

At the start of his career, he was an opening act for the likes of Bette Davis and Humphrey Bogart. Today he's a headliner.

Leonard Maltin on Bugs Bunny's 50th birthday

Bugs [Bunny] seems to embody just what we are—or just what we like to think we are, and that's allowed in the symbolism biz. He's plucky, free-thinking and ingenious. A self-reliant Joe with a wisecrack, always ready to take the huffing, puffing heavies of the world down a notch or two.

Steve O'Donnell

What's up doc?
Good news! You're in great shape for a 50-year-old! Great cardio-vascular efficiency; low cholesterol; low body fat. Terrific muscle flexibility! A perfect vegetarian diet! Keep it up, Bugs! You'll last forever.

From a cartoon by Edward Koren

Ted Turner's Fonda Jane.

Article headline in LA TIMES

When I hear about another Elvis sighting, it gives me a headache.

Priscilla Presley

He got up and left because everyone was looking at him, and then the youngsters pounced on his table grabbing the water glass and other items the star had touched.

Jason Stromme commenting on seeing Bruce Willis at a ski lodge in Leavenworth, Washington

Jane Pauley didn't want to be thought of as a one-trick pony . . . people seem to think that Jane had no clue of what was going on until she started reading about it in the papers. Jane knew. Before it happened, Jane knew. . . . Jane had to find out that Jane had a future at NBC.

Jane Pauley

If she wasn't married, I'm sure we would have been married now. . . . But she was very happily married and still is.

Actor Raymond Burr, television's Perry Mason, revealing his true feelings for his co-star Barbara Hale

They're a very wholesome, all American group that has the same kind of family values that McDonald's has.

David Greene of the McDonald Corporation on New Kids on the Block

That I had an affair with David Letterman. I wish it were true. He's so shy and private. I think he uses Corn Husker's Lotion.

Comedian Sandra Bernhard, asked by SPIN magazine to name her favorite rumor about herself

Madonna's lyrics speak about issues relevant to young women today: unplanned pregnancy, disillusionment with traditional views of marriage, an abusive father. She also includes a fact sheet about AIDS and a toll-free number to call for more information inside her "Like a Prayer" CD.

Teresa M. Becker

I admire her so much. She's like a breast with a boom box.

Comedian Judy Tenuta on Madonna

She's letting her aging Boy Toy think he still has it. The one thing she really wants is a successful movie career, and Warren can give it to her.

A close observer

. . . As for ambition, she makes Streisand look squishy.

Liz Smith, gossip columnist, on Madonna

Madonna must have the most valuable bust in the business. What if she had an allergic reaction to the glue? What if we discolor a breast or inflict some kind of permanent damage? Not only will we be sued, we'll become known as the two schmucks who destroyed a national treasure.

DICK TRACY makeup man John Caglione describing his thankless task of having to glue down Madonna's breasts to keep them from popping out of their Breathless Mahoney outfit

Sometimes I think, he's been with the world's most beautiful, most glamorous, talented women. I go, "Oh, my God! Oh, my God!". . . . I mean how can I ever be as fabulous as Brigitte Bardot when she was 25. Or Natalie Wood. . . . Then there is the other side of me that says I'm better than all of them.

Madonna talking to VANITY FAIR about Warren Beatty's past love affairs

Madonna is simultaneously touching and more fun than a barrel of monkeys. She's funny, and she's gifted in so many areas and has the kind of energy as a performer that can't help but make you engaged.

Warren Beatty

They [Madonna and Warren Beatty] were always kissing each other. It was embarrassing and awkward for the crew.

An unknown observer

The film is Warren's dream come true. Every other actor is as ugly as sin, and he looks just beautiful.

Actor Paul Sorvino on Warren Beatty as Dick Tracy

If kids knew him, it was mainly as Madonna's 53-year-old boyfriend.

Critic Richard Corliss

[I caught him] in bed with men several times. In fact, one of the best times, I caught him in bed with Mick Jagger.

Angela Bowie, former wife of singer David Bowie

I was one of the weird guys who did music and one of the guys who never could get a girlfriend. Because I was not into girls.

Singer Lenny Kravitz

AND SO FORTH

I can't say that we're really great friends—we don't have a helluva lot in common—but we'll always be connected like brother and sister. That helps when the romance comes and goes.

Valerie Bertinelli on husband Eddie Van Halen

Women who live alone spend only half of what bachelors spend on entertainment but they spend it more than many men on pets, toys, playground equipment, and other home-centered entertainment products.

Thomas Exter

The realm of comedy and cartoons has been shaped by males. In many cases, mother-in-law jokes are actually aimed at their wives.

Anthropologist Alan Ehrlic

A lot of serious theater is like bad church—you have to be uncomfortable sitting there for three hours and be talked down to.

Playwright Mary Myers

[Lambada dancing] is about the closest you can get to having sex without actually doing it.

Los Angeles dance instructor Michael Davis

We hate critics. . . . Most of them are fat and ugly and they criticize.

Milli Vanilli

It's great to be a sex symbol. I grew up wishing the girls would really like me, and now people ask me what I feel like being a sex symbol. Are you crazy? It's dope! I love it! It's fun and it's not like it's gone to my head and I suddenly think I'm sexy 'cause I got zits.

20-year-old Donnie Wahlberg of New Kids on the Block

A photographer has a more dangerous weapon than a gun. It doesn't kill—it wounds for life.

Photographer Norman Parkinson

Beam up: Get high on crack.
Pop junk: Gossip.
Dis: show disrespect.

From SLANG: WORDS AND TERMS by Peter Commanday

More young Americans today love humor if it is gruesome, targets women, or is low-key

According to a study of collegians by James Carroll, a psychology professor at Central Michigan University

The media don't really give young people role models anymore. Now you get role models like Donald Trump and all the moneymakers—no one with real ideals.

Christina Chinn

Chapter 9

RELIGION

CATHOLICS

Where Catholics are perceived not only as treating Church teaching on abortion with contempt, but helping to multiply abortions by advocating legislation supporting abortion, or by making public funds available for abortion, bishops may decide that, for the common good, such Catholics must be warned that they are at risk of excommunication.

New York's John Cardinal O'Connor

This is redolent of another era. It's like an outbreak of polio; we thought we had it conquered. This document comes out of the church of the 1940s and 1950s. The document is not a surprise; it's an embarrassment.

University of Notre Dame's theology department chairman commenting on the Vatican's "Instruction on the Ecclesial Vocation of the Theologian" which severely limits the freedom of theologians

The most hopeful sign I see for the near future of the Catholic Church is:

". . . the people leaving it."

". . . the gutsy missionaries abroad."

". . . the Blessed Mother appearing at Medjugorje [Yugo-
slavia]."

". . . Dorothy Day, the Martyrs of Latin America, Mother
Teresa, Father Daniel Berrigan . . ."

From a survey conducted by U.S. CATHOLIC MAGAZINE

The church's formal teaching is still in opposition to birth
control, but the vast majority of Catholics have departed
from that position and approve of and participate in birth
control practices.

Sociologist James Davidson

The major conflict within the [Catholic] church in this century is between those church leaders who object to married
Catholics enjoying sex and the laity, whose insights tells
them that sexual love is good, that it is meant to be enjoyed,
that it binds men and women together and heals the wounds
of the common life.

Andrew Greeley

People who encounter discrimination against Catholics tend
to be shocked that it still exists today. It's not a tremen-
dously widespread or vicious problem, but it is still here.

Michael Schwartz, director of the Center for Catholic Policy

The complicated thing about the relationships between
priests and women was that often the only man who would
listen to a woman was a priest. He had to. Sacramentally,
he had to listen to you in confession. That was a kind of
luxury, and it opened up the possibility for discourse between men and women.

Novelist Mary Gordon

The Catholic Church is sacrificing people to maintain the
marriage bond. The bishops also find the church guilty of
urging women to "offer" unlimited and often unconditional
forgiveness and perpetual reconciliation. Titled "The Heritage of Violence" the document goes on to say that perpetual reconciliation in the name of a mystical state . . . is

very difficult to attain. There are cases where the marriage bond no longer makes any sense.

The working draft by the Social Affairs Committee of the
Quebec Assembly of Catholic Bishops

The Vatican's obsession with sex is a world-wide scandal that demonstrates a serious psychic imbalance.

Theologian Matthew Fox

PROTESTANT RELIGION

"Megachurches"—churches which 2000 or more people attend each week. "Pop gospel," "fast-food theology," "fast-food religion," "McChurch."

Terms used to describe new churches that feature high-tech
entertainment, daycare, self-help groups

A jury has awarded $500,000 to a Jehovah's Witness couple in Antioch [California], who said their 3-1/2-year-old child was given a blood transfusion against their wishes during a kidney transplant.

Staff and wire reports

The 10 most favorite hymns:
1. "Amazing Grace"
2. "How Great Thou Art"
3. "In the Garden"
4. "The Old Rugged Cross"
5. "What a Friend I Have in Jesus"
6. "A Mighty Fortress"
7. "Blessed Assurance"
8. "He Lives"
9. "Victory in Jesus"
10. "Holy, Holy, Holy"

According to the
Newspaper Enterprise Association

There are 3 bishops, 47 district superintendents, and 2975 pastors for a total of 3,025 women clergy serving currently in the United Methodist Church alone.

The Reverend Ms. Morey Y.J. Aleona

The percentage of American adults who considered themselves "born again" has held steady at 34% over the past seven years, but, due to the increase in the adult American population, the actual number of born again believers has increased to 60 million.

According to the Barna Research Group

The holy war is over. The Fundamentalists have won. We're fixing to enter the darkest period in our history.

Southern Baptist Editor Jack U. Harwell on the election of Reverend Morris Chapman as president of the Southern Baptist Convention

[The Bakker's] personify the most characteristic excesses of the 1980s—the greed, the love of goods, and the shamelessness. . . . To this list could be added narcissism, the characteristic disease of the age.

Frances FitzGerald

Latin American evangelicals are more likely to behave like a good-government lobby than an anticommunist crusade. They are best understood as a cultural revitalization movement. Having originated as a reformation in personal morality, evangelicals are now groping for ways to reform public morality.

David Stoll, author of IS LATIN AMERICA TURNING PROTESTANT?

THE BIBLE

If they ever targeted literature, the Bible would be the first book that would require a label. It's full of people [having sex], killing each other, God's vengeful wrath,

Eve with her snakes and apples—that's all pretty lusty stuff. I'd hate to see the Bible get banned. I think it's a pretty nice book.

Rocker Gene Simmons of Kiss

A sampling verses from the newly re-translated Revised Standard Bible:

"What are human beings that you are mindful of them, mortals that you care for them?"
Psalm 8:4, New Revised Standard Bible, 1990

"What is man that thou are mindful of him, and the son of man that thou dost care for him?"
Psalm 8:4, Revised Standard Bible, 1952

"A wind from God swept over the face of the waters."
Genesis 1:2, New Revised Standard Bible, 1990

"The Spirit of God was moving over the face of the waters."
Genesis 1:2, Revised Standard Bible, 1952

"There is also one mediator between God and humankind, Christ Jesus, himself human."
1 Timothy 2:5, New Revised Standard Bible, 1990

"There is one mediator between God and men, the man Christ Jesus."
1 Timothy 2:5, Revised Standard Bible, 1952

Today I started re-reading the Bible—and I'm traumatized!

Caption from a cartoon

The U.S. Supreme Court ruled unanimously that states could tax Bibles and similar religious goods sold through the mail or at evangelistic crusades. This is not [a tax on the right to disseminate religious information, ideas or beliefs], but are merely neutral taxes on "the privilege of making retail sales of tangible personal property."

As reported by NEWSWEEK

JESUS

Have Jesus—will share

Bumper sticker

Jesus was an African

T-shirt

My boss is a Jewish carpenter

Bumper sticker

Jesus would probably not even use a [surfboard]. He'd probably go out there and ride the waves in his bare feet.

According to surfer and minister James Gould

If Jesus personally asked me to sell everything and follow him, I would:

"Not do such a silly thing."
"Realistically, I don't think he would."
"I would, but I would ask him to take care of my wife."
"Perhaps he has already asked and, not recognizing him, I have not followed."
"I can do Christ's work a lot better as I am now than I could if I had nothing."

A sampling of responses from a survey conducted by
U.S. CATHOLIC MAGAZINE

Jesus was not crucified for saying or doing what made sense to everyone.

Stanley Hauerwas and William H. Willimon

AND SO FORTH

If, after 2 millennia of estrangement and hostility, Christians and Jews can create a genuine culture of mutual self-esteem and reciprocal caring, [it] could be a sign and an inspiration of hope to other religions, races, and ethnic groups. . . .

Rabbi Marc H. Tanenbaum

No individual should have to suffer and die because of the religious beliefs of another.

Jetta Bernier

Just as men have been criticized for excluding women's experience from theology, feminists justifiably have been called to account for failing to recognize that white women's experiences are not the same as that of blacks and other minorities.

June Christine Goudey

. . . Symptomatic of our society's sickness: that it knows no divine commandment nor desires any sanctification; that it seeks life apart from God, who is the soul's source of life; that it searches for freedom but is unwilling to bear the cross; that it wants a story to look like, but will not teach or learn the One Story.

Theologian Elizabeth Achtemeier

Pay mind to your own life, your own health, and wholeness. A bleeding heart is of no help to anyone if it bleeds to death.

Novelist Frederick Buechner

Black folk expect the preacher to reassure them of God's power, not to question or doubt it. They expect the pastor to help them cope with joblessness, poverty and discrimination by transforming their despair into hope. Black theology needs to provide the content and method for changing the social, economic and political obstacles for blacks.

Pastor James Henry Harris

African-American theology began when the first slave wondered about a God whose followers kept people in chains while calling them "brothers and sisters."

Gayraud Wilmore

Churches that are closed systems are so insecure that they believe their survival depends on destroying everything that differs from them or does not support them. Such churches lack faith in the gospels inherent power.

Anne Wilson Schaef

Theological or denominational differences are not at the core of [the abortion] dispute. Rather, the primary issue at stake among the churches is a philosophical question: What is the nature of human life and which philosophical concepts most adequately depicted?

Professor Mark Ellingsen

A Superior Court judge in San Diego has ruled that clergy are not exempted from a California law that requires health practitioners, child care custodians, and employees of child protective agencies to report knowledge of possible child-molestation cases.

As reported in the CHRISTIAN CENTURY

Although God demands a whole heart, he will accept a broken one if he gets all the pieces.

From "Pulpit Helps"

Helping others, that's the main thing. The only way for us to help ourselves is to help others and to listen to each others' stories.

Writer Elie Wiesel, reflecting on the Holocaust

This book helped me see that the things I do that I identify as "good" behavior, the "right" thing, the "virtuous" deed are not always such. Often they are a cover for not being fully honest, for playing the martyr, for subtly manipulating other people.

Fr. Martin J. Kirk on CO-DEPENDENCE *by Anne Wilson Schaef*

The world's Christian population grew by some 326 million during the past decade to 1,758,777,900, or about 33 percent of the world population. There are 963 million Roman Catholics, 324 million Protestants, 180 million Orthodox and 54 million Anglicans.

> *According to David Barrett in the INTERNATIONAL BULLETIN OF MISSIONARY RESEARCH*

There are now more Muslims than Methodists both in Britain and in the United States; and it is estimated that within three years there will be more Muslims than Jews in the U.S.

> *Colin Chapman*

An effective Christian Education program has the strongest ties to a person's growth in faith and to loyalty to one's congregation or denomination.

> *According to a study by the Search Institute*

The one TV program that has nourished my faith is:

"Star Trek."
"60 Minutes." It makes me pray more for people.
"The Brady Bunch" was a caring family show with high ideals.
"Family Ties." . . . The characters acted toward each other in a Christian way.
"Rescue 911." It tells me that there are good people who really care about others.

> *A sampling of responses from a survey conducted by U.S. CATHOLIC*

Today, more than at any other time, there are pharasaical phonies . . . who salve their consciences not by giving their own money away but by advocating that the United States government give away everyone else's.

> *Thomas F. Roeser*

Why is prayer so neglected? It reflects our general fear of intimacy, which is in turn responsible for our lack of deep friendships, and indeed for the whole undernourishment of relational life.

> *Professor James M. Houston*

God is bread when you're hungry, water when you're thirsty, a harbor from the storm. God's a father to the fatherless, a mother to the motherless. God's my sister, my brother, my leader, my guide, my teacher, my comforter, my friend. . . . Some people see these [images] as contradictory, but Christians see them as inadequate.

Sister Thea Bowman

The problems, hurts, and difficulties that will definitely result from legalized drugs will be far, far less numerous and less destructive to the whole society than the theft, bribery, violence, murder, mayhem and self-degradation that are the daily bread in the U.S. today.

Father John Clifton Marquis, on legalizing all drugs

Please come, God, take good care of yourself. If anything should happen to you, we are all sunk.

From Ann Landers' column

Billy Graham will be the 1,900th star on the famed sidewalk on Hollywood Boulevard, near those of Julie Andrews and Wayne Newton.

As reported in TIME

The life-story itself, when told honestly, carries a holiness within it. . . .That holiness speaks to the yearning that is in everybody's heart for holiness with a capital H.

Sister Mary Irving

But who is our neighbor? In relation to health care, Canadians answered the question by saying that every permanent resident within their borders was a neighbor. Thus, mercy became a national priority.

Reverend Everett L. Wilson

The word "altruism" offends me. Caring for others without due respect for the self does not make a better world; unless we understand our own needs we cannot know the needs of others.

Mary Lou Wright

I am not a prostitute. What I am guilty of is believing in a religion that is very advanced for its time.

Mary Ellen Tracy who had sex with hundreds of men as high priestess of an ancient Egyptian religion

Anywhere from 3 million to 10 million people currently participate in the 2500 to 5000 cult organizations in the U.S.

William Kent Bintner, assistant director of the Positive Action Center

Maybe God could use the dollar more than the scholar.

Commodities trader Mark Ritchie on why he left the seminary

TV is not just a vast wasteland; it is a toxic-waste dump. The problem is not that nothing is there; that would be bad enough. The problem is that something is there and it's poisonous to the spirit.

James Brieg

Insofar as teaching about different faiths helps citizens live in an ethically and religiously plural democracy, public schools are required by various state constitutions to provide it. A sympathetic understanding of other faiths is plainly necessary to enable adults to promote equality and exercise sound political judgment.

Professor Timothy L. Smith

When mercy becomes a business, giving only some people access to basic services while others are denied for no better reason than lack of money, it stinks of privilege. And when anything stinks, it is a summons to change.

Reverend Everett L. Wilson

Consider that in the same year [1987] Americans spent almost the same amount—$1.7 billion—on Nintendo, as was spent on world missions.

Sylvia Ronsvalles

In a mail survey of 80 pastors conducted by Ronald Barton and the Reverend Karen Lebacqz for the Center for Ethics and Social Policy approximately 10% said they had a relationship with a church member.

Associated Press

LUVS GOD

California license plate

Sellers desperate to unload houses are turning to divine intervention—burying statues of St. Joseph in their yards.

Unknown news story

I believe, says McClean, Virginia, mortgage banker Sheila Borland, who handed out dozens of $1 statues to agents—and ten houses sold within six weeks.

From WHAT'S NEXT

The church should be a forum for debate, rather than issue mandates and wonder why people don't follow them.

Reverend Alan Houghton

Accepting responsibility for our lives is the most thrilling thing with which we can ever come to terms.

Betty Bethards

The issue is not sexual abuse, . . . it is the abuse of power. Clergy who symbolically represent God and the Church always have more power than the parishioners they approach for sexual affairs.

Journalist Diane Weddington, quoting the Reverend Marie Fortune, author of IS NOTHING SACRED: WHEN SEX INVADES THE PASTORAL RELATIONSHIP

God loves you and I'm trying

Bumper sticker

Monogamy is as unnatural as celibacy. If people want to try, O.K., but the fact is, people are not monogamous. It is crazy to hold up this ideal and pretend it's what we're doing and we're not.

J. Robert Williams, the first openly gay Episcopal priest

Tough times don't last, tough people do.

Evangelist Robert Schuller

Nothing will change until you take action to change yourself.

Ra Bonewitz

Now that I have distance from it, I can see there is a passion and mystery, even a discipline, that's very beautiful about religion.

Madonna

A religion for losers.

Ted Turner, owner of Cable News Network, on Christianity

That was a very uncalled-for statement. At one time or another, I have offended just about everybody. I was making a talk off the cuff when it just popped out, and I feel very sorry for it.

Ted Turner apologizing

To be upset over what you don't have is to waste what you do have.

Ken Keyes, Jr.

None of your articles addressed God's use of animal skins in the Bible. I find it difficult to feel guilty when I follow the pattern established by Yahweh.

Reverend Timothy L. Munyon

Seventy-five percent of American women and 62% of American men believe in miracles.

According to the BRUSKIN REPORT

The God idea has caused more harm to the human race, all other species of every animal, every other living organism, and even the basic earth itself than all other ideas together which have been formulated, institutionalized, and acted upon by humankind.

Madalyn O'Hair, founder of American Atheists

Chapter 10

SCIENCE

GENERAL SCIENCE

Each year, nearly 4 million replacement body parts are installed in human beings.

Jerome C. Glenn

Today, the success of plastics recycling programs is not limited by technology, but, rather, by the availability of the plastics from the consumer. We need to educate society that plastics don't have to be an environmental villain.

David Spencer

It is now possible to convert inedible vegetable waste, stalks, stems, leaves and woody materials into ethanol, a clean burning fuel which can be used to reduce air pollution and our need for foreign oil.

Professor Lonnie O. Ingram

Technology is rapidly out-stripping the public's ability to comprehend [so many] changes.

Steven Lindow

How are we going to compete in a high technology world when we are turning out students who can't figure percentages and don't know what gravity is?

Lee Iacocca

Contrary to the old warning that time waits for no one, time slows down when you are on the move. . . . If you could move about the speed of light, 186,282 miles per second, your time would stand still. If you could move faster than light, outpacing your shadow, your time would move backwards.

Mark Davidson

We've removed 50% of the sulfur from coal by dissolving it with bacterial enzymes in an unusually prepared emulsion. . . . Coal desulfurization is likely to become increasingly important because, while oil supplies are limited, the world has enough coal to last three or four centuries

Professor Teh Fu Yen

We just beginning to realize that pathogenic bacteria can sense their surroundings so they know when they're in a setting in which they could cause disease.

Brett Finlay

As the [Hubble] telescope's 2.4-meter primary mirror was being polished in 1980 and 1981, explained NASA officials, an unrecognized 1-millimeter error in the structure of the device used to monitor the process caused the technicians to give the mirror an exquisitely smooth surface with a grossly inaccurate shape. The result is the "spherical aberration" that now bathes the stars in fuzz whenever Hubble tries to look at them.

N. Mitchel Waldrop

A new million-Swiss-franc biomedical prize, the Helmut Horten Research Award. The international award, worth about $710,000, intends to honor achievements and to encourage further research in the field of medicine or biology of benefit to human health.

After more than eighty years modern physics has learned to live comfortably with one of its fundamental tenets: no particle, no signal, no causal connection . . . can travel faster than *c*, the speed of light in a vacuum . . . 299,792,458 meters a second.

Alan Burdick

A pathologist once told me that indoor plumbing, with the subsequent control of diseases like typhoid, was the greatest medical achievement. Add the discovery of antiseptics, antibiotics, anesthesia, and vaccination, and we have the core of the modern medical health miracle.

Pat Wagner

The Big Bang model [of the origin of the universe] suffers from crucial failures that are becoming increasingly serious with continuing progress in astronomical observations. The observations, however, are consistent with a universe that is unlimited in time and space. . . . It is clear that God did not limit himself to a finite universe at one time and place, but made the universe in his own image, infinite in space and time.

Dr. Paul Marmet, Canadian Institute of Astrophysics

NASA's Magellan spacecraft successfully entered orbit around Venus last week, and is now on course for its mission to map the planet.

NEW SCIENTIST

Wouldn't it be funny if there was nothing wrong with the [Hubble] telescope at all. It is just that the whole universe was fuzzy.

Comedian Jay Leno

Biological meltdown—The effect on the earth of acid rain, air pollution, ozone depletion, water loss, toxic wastes, greenhouse effect, etc.

Charles Manes

Ted Turner cares very deeply about the declining standards on this planet and the degradation of the environment. So he thought that if we asked the dreamers of the world for solutions, then maybe solutions would show up.

Tom Guinzburg on the half-million-dollar
"Turner Tomorrow Award"

The scientific theory I like is that the rings of Saturn are composed entirely of lost airline luggage.

Mark Russell

The shape of the earth resembles a slightly crushed potato rather than a ball.

According to a study by West German and
Swiss scientists

SCIENTISTS AT WORK

The National Science Foundation predicts that, by the year 2006, the U.S. will have a cumulative shortfall of 675,000 people with bachelor's degrees in natural science and engineering.

According to the American Chemical Society

Scientists at the Sandia National Laboratory in New Mexico are working on prototypes of a 1,800-foot-long cannon that will literally shoot small payloads into orbit, using electromagnetic force as a propellant [instead of rocket fuels].

George Nobbe

The whole trick about being a scientist or an artist is being able to re-engage with the ordinary. That's where the good stuff is. It is right in front of your nose all the time. The fresh look with a different perspective is going to do 90% of the work.

Computer whiz Alan Kay

Worrying about things that no one else worries about is where insights come from.

Physicist Roger Penrose

Recently, armed with only a pair of binoculars mounted on pipes, optical technician Don Machholz discovered what may be one of the most unusual comets known, long before professional astronomers noticed it. . . . Comet Machholz has an unusually short orbit around the sun—a mere 5.3 years as compared with the 76 years for Halley's Comet.

Mark Sunlin

I'm wondering if great geneticists have considered the staggering negative effects that could result from seemingly grand discoveries, such as a cure for Alzheimer's disease or cancer. The population would skyrocket. . . . The overpopulation that would result would be a problem that would overshadow all of the diseases combined, many times over.

Jeff St. Laurent

In socialist regimes many famous physicists or natural scientists have been involved in human rights because science always requires independent thought.

Chinese dissident and astrophysicist, Fang Lizhi

My heart leapt. I quickly cut out more hexagons and pentagons, pasted them together, and magically at the end I had one pentagon and a pentagonal hole in the top. Eureka. When Harry [Kroto] saw it the next day, he was taken with the beauty of it.

Chemist Rick Smalley describing the discovery of the structure of carbon$_{60}$

[Zoologist George Bittner] has already successfully reconnected both ends of the worm's severed nerves by dipping them in a chemical substance called polyethylene glycol. . . . If the process is successful with rats, it could be used to repair human nerve damage within two years.

Russell M. Nelson

ANIMALS AND HUMANS

A bat's sonar is so finely tuned that it can detect something
as thin as a hair, including its width, texture, and change
of position.

Professor Barry Keller

We know that most children with birth defects do not inherit
them from either parent. Most defects result from new mu-
tations in germ cells—the cells that develop into sperm or
eggs.

Professor Bruce W. Kovacs

If all mankind were to disappear, the world would regen-
erate back to the rich state of equilibrium that existed 10,000
years ago. If insects were to vanish, the environment would
collapse into chaos.

Entomologist Edward O. Wilson

The vast majority of American Indians most likely de-
scended from a single migrating population from Asia.

Biochemist Douglas C. Wallace

Now scientists have a much clearer idea of how underarm
odors arise: The apocrine gland in the armpit makes secretions. Microscopic bacteria thrive on the secretions. After
devouring the secretions, the bacteria expel 3-methyl-2-
hexenoic acid. And the nose knows the rest of the story.

Tim Friend

Tokyo-based Shimizu Corporation, the world's largest construction company, is planning an orbiting 64-room hotel,
designed to accommodate 100 guests 270 miles above the
planet. [It is] scheduled for the year 2020.

Steve Nadis

The garbage glut has prompted thousands of parents to
toss their disposable diapers and turn back to cloth. Their
environmental awareness has fueled a rebirth for diaper

services in hospitals and homes, sending revenues up 38.5% last year, to $250 million.

Naushad S. Mehta

The 8,800 known species of the family Formicidae [ants] make up from 10% to 15% of the world's animal biomass, the total weight of all fauna. They are the most dominant social insect in the world, found almost everywhere except in the polar regions.

Journalist R.Z. Sheppard

Dolphins are not that discriminatory. They'll get it on with just about anything, and it doesn't have to be alive. People may think it an honor, but actually they'll do it with a drainpipe.

Ecologist Georgia Cranmore, on the sexual proclivities of dolphins

High-achieving math people are somewhat more outgoing than the average person. . . . In fact, they are solid, confident, well-adjusted people.

Analyst Michael Shaughnessy

COMPUTERS

From "The Ten Commandments of Networking":
1. Thou shalt acquire a network if thine employees spend more time searching for information than working with it
2. Thou shalt not covet thy neighbor's costly system; purchase only to meet thine needs.
3. Thou shalt choose a network with great popularity so that thou canst acquire advanced software in the future.

Steve Kaplan

A lot of people believe one way to get rid of [computer] hacking might be to eliminate computer security. With no reason to figure something out, there's no temptation to break in.

Keith Bostic

The student who caused the computer virus that disrupted the nation's entire interconnected computer network received a sentence of three years probation. The student went home and immediately programmed the overturn of his sentence.

Comedian Mark Russell

The computer power that sent a man to the moon twenty years ago is now on each of your desks. The computer power of the first Univac, almost 40 years ago, is now in your wristwatch.

Everett N. Ehrlich, QUOTE magazine

The very fact that the mind leads us to truths that are not computable convinces me that a computer can never duplicate the mind.

Physicist Roger Penrose

PRODUCTS AND PROCESSES

Quasi-crystals
> *A new form of matter whose existence was confirmed this year. They fall between amorphous solids like glass and crystals and rocks and minerals*

Receptor Message Watch
> *At $275, it can signal its wearer to call the office, phone home or dial a specific number displayed on the face.*

[Biodegradable products] foster precisely the wrong attitude. . . . They foster the idea that throwing stuff away is a good idea.

Environmental Defense Fund spokesman Jim Middaugh

Alpha-Stin-CS
> *An electro-medical device used in addiction therapy to release endorphins into one's brain and induce an alpha state. Popular among Hollywood types.*

Scientists have created the microscopic equivalent of a trac-
tor beam [called "optical tweezers"] that can catch and manipulate living objects without touching them and without
causing obvious damage.

Dr. John Grauerholz

Compared with the [new Honda Acura] NSX, a Chevrolet
Corvette felt like it was from the Iron Age. A Ferrari 328
felt ponderous, massively challenging to drive, and not ter-
ribly quick.

AUTOMOBILE

Silica aerogel is amazingly light; a chunk the size of a brick
weighs less than a paperclip. Yet it's so strong it can support
1,600 times its own weight.

Greg Pope

Cold fusion is a hoax produced by a psychological disorder
of self-deception.

According to Professor Robert Crease and N. P. Saimos,
as reported in 21ST CENTURY SCIENCE AND TECHNOLOGY

Any qualified scientist who studies the latest scientific literature on cold fusion must now accept cold fusion as a
new physical principal.

Engineer Hal Fox

An increase of 1.5 miles per gallon in the fuel efficiency of
American automobiles would save as much oil as the US
imported from Iraq and Kuwait last year.

According to the Natural Resources Defense Council

"The Bug Beater"—a giant vacuum cleaner that goes
through the fields and sucks bugs right off plants, and which
could reduce the need for pesticides.

Built by Sukup Manufacturing Company

Chapter 11

SOCIETY

SEX

I know I'm not Mr. Right, but . . . would you settle for Mr. Right Now?

From "Quigmans" cartoons

Clothes aren't sexy, women are.

Japanese designer Issey Miyake

Do you carve your jack-o'-lanterns with a mean or happy face?

Winner of the St. Pauli Girl contest in 1989 for the most clever come-on line

The lambada is essentially choreographed sex.

Movie critic Joe Baltake

This shows that the sexual behavior of Americans is more circumspect and traditional than the libertine impression we get from the popular media and fiction.

Tom W. Smith, director of a survey revealing the average U.S. adult has sex once a week

Borrowing from the tango and merengue, lambada is a fast-paced dance performed with the man's right leg placed between the thighs of his partner.

TIME

But the hardest part was telling my parents about the pictures. I cried, told them I was sorry. They said there was nothing to be sorry about.

Vanessa Williams talking about losing the Miss America crown in 1984 after PENTHOUSE ran nude photos of her

Couples who have violent relationships, common interests or several children tend to have sex more often than other couples.

From a study by sociologist Denise Donnelly

It's easier to develop a perfectly good sexual relationship between two people who are caring, intimate, and respectful friends than to develop that kind of a friendship between two people who are madly in love with one another.

Dr. Sol Gordon

The clinical definition of low sexual desire, now called hypoactive sexual desire (HSD) by therapists, is engaging in sexual activity (including masturbation) or having sexual thoughts, fantasies or urges less than twice a month.

Daniel Goleman

If you don't feel like making love, don't say "no," say "I love you and I love making love with you, but I'm so wiped out. How about tomorrow?"

Dr. Alan Say

Studies indicate that black adolescents compared with white adolescents are younger at first coitus, are more likely to have unprotected sex, and that the average age black boys start having sex is 12.

Dr. Loretta Sweet-Jemmott

Sex is suddenly once again the unmentionable, and one wonders if that's going to lead to more right-wing thinking and to a kind of f——g depressing grayness to the quality of life. It's returned everything that we despised in the early 60s.

David Bowie

A strong sexual appetite, an ability to separate emotion from sex, an aptitude for solving logistical problems, and a strong sense of self.

The characteristics of women who can handle long-term sexual liaisons according to Susan Crain Bakos

[Most people in sex addiction programs] are normal people who are thinking, feeling or doing sexual things they don't like. Control for them is not impossible, just emotionally painful. A sophisticated therapist would explore why that's so.

Sex therapist Marty Klein

If after lovemaking [he] stays awake, talks tenderly, and promises to call . . . he is married.

Dorian Yaeger

I'd like to put on buckskins and a ponytail and go underwater with a reed, hiding from the Indians. I'd love to be pushing off a birchbark canoe in a forest. To me, that's sexy!

Kevin Costner

THE SEXES

Things that attract a person to the opposite sex:
1. A caring and considerate nature
2. A good sense of humor
3. Having compatible interests
4. Being a good conversationalist
5. Intelligence

6. Being a good sex partner
7. Being romantic
According to a survey conducted by PARENTS MAGAZINE

Of developments to free women from enslavement, the invention of pantyhose has to rate among the top ten.

Jill Johnson Piper on the 30th anniversary of the discovery of pantyhose

Men growing up are rewarded socially for eating a lot.

Ryan Casey

Food in the hands of a woman is considered good when she gives it to somebody else and bad when she eats it herself.

Elizabeth Gleick

. . . Paris haute couture—a tradition of custom-fitted dressmaking geared to 3,000 ladies able to spend $35,000 or so on a single dress.

PEOPLE

Three out of ten watchers of daytime soap operas are men.

L. M. Boyd

Within the last 20 years or so, a strong social movement has provided women to be more expressive in the area of anger. The passive nature so long nurtured by society has given way to more natural aggressive drives that have always been in women.

Psychologist George H. Guthrey

Middle age begins at 46 and ends at 65.

According to a study by the American Board of Family Practice

On average, today's man spends 45 minutes each day on personal grooming, up from 30 minutes a day in 1988.

According to GQ *magazine*

I'm probably the only model in New York who hasn't had breast implants.

Model Kim Alexis

The dominant silhouette at the Paris fall collections was a big top with tights or leggings, often accompanied by boots that climbed well above the knee. In between there was often a sort of apron that resembled a vestigial skirt or, more fancifully, a superwide belt.

Journalist Martha Duffy

Research shows that young men flirt differently than young women. Males are much more tuned into the physical aspects of relationship, while females more to establishing friendship.

As reported by Professor Barbara Montgomery

My kids watch "Teenage Mutant Ninja Turtles" and "He-Man and the Masters of the Universe" because these shows portray females in nontraditional roles. The women in these programs are strong, brave, understanding and highly competent, and most of the males treat them with respect. Anyone who doesn't gets his comeuppance.

Wyn L. Lydecker

Success is more than knowing how. It's knowing when.

Advertisement for hair-growth formula Rogaine

In a recent study, the drug Cyoctol produced significant hair growth in ten of twelve balding men—that's better than the 30% success rate reported for Minoxidil.

Jonathan Bor

Be responsible within your sexual role, and transcend it with understanding, not denial.

Steve Stiles

The cavemen went out scavaging together side-by-side, but they had to keep quiet so as to not scare off their prey.

They became close by *doing*. The women, on the other hand, were gatherers and stayed in one place. Face-to-face conversation was an important part of interaction and it also served to keep prey away. They became close by *being*.

Anthropologist Helen Fisher

The beauty queen from hell.

Nickname for newly crowned Miss Universe, Mona Grudt, who hails from Hell, Norway

Fifty percent of the women polled by the Roper Organization agreed that men are more interested in their own, rather than a woman's, sexual satisfaction—up from 40% in 1970.

As reported by LADIES HOME JOURNAL

Women who are built for comfort, not speed—Delta Burke, Ricki Lake, Marianne Sagebrecht.

According to ESQUIRE

Forty-two percent of the women polled . . . believe men are basically selfish and self-centered—up from 32% in 1970.

According to the Roper Organization

Women want men to be strong, capable, paternal, and at the same time compassionate, vulnerable, yielding.

Dr. Mara Gleckel-Mathan, Director of Women's Counseling Service of New York

"Stud Muffin," "Stud Puppy," "Killer."

Nicknames for fit and muscular men in various parts of the country

Woman of the Year—The real Laura Palmer: 23-year-old actress, Cheryl Lee.

ESQUIRE

The fashion industry has to change to fit working women. For baby boomer's, quality is much more important than price.

Beate Ziegert

The careers held by Barbie, the doll, since 1959 (in chronological order):
   Fashion model
   Ballerina
   Stewardess
   Candy striper
   Teacher
   Fashion editor
   Flight attendant
   Medical doctor
   Olympic athlete
   Aerobics instructor
   TV news reporter
   Fashion designer
   Corporate executive
   Perfume designer
   Animal rights volunteer

According to Mattel, the company that created Barbie

My situation is central to a lot of women of my generation. We were encouraged to be professional. The whole deal with men and babies—you didn't even *mention* it. That was going to be later. And now it is later. It's a lot later.

Comedian Lauri Anderson

With men and boys at home your bathroom needs cleaning every day.

From an ad from Lysol Bathroom Touch-Ups

The beer-gut has been disgraced in favor of an unfogged mind, unimpaired driving ability and, best of all, a waist.

Andrew Bill commenting on popularity of non-alcoholic beers

MARRIAGE

. . . The couples who were able to set aside an evening a week, during which they could put their kids to bed early or get a babysitter and go out for a walk or talk about the things they have in common or make love, were the couples who were best able to cope with the normal stresses they encountered. It is important to find quality time with kids, but it's more important to the family as a whole to find quality time with your partner.

Psychologist David Olson

Most men cheat and a lot of women do. It's not a reason to get a divorce.

Helen Gurley Brown

For women marrying younger men, the divorce rates are 56% higher than average.

Sociologist Neil Bennett

Women who take husbands' names see themselves as progressive, not as traditional in some "Ozzie and Harriet" mold. It's important to the family identity to have one name.

Gay Bomier

I'm glad I [kept my family name]. Even if it is only a symbolic gesture at first, it leads to mental and emotional balance in a healthy marriage.

Kimberlee J. Remus

As you become more successful, you have to deal with the trappings of success: money, mortgages, ex-wives. . . . I have a Mercedes and a BMW and a new pool and a Jacuzzi . . . and I don't mind champagne. But those things can come and go. I don't really care about them. I think I've remained a hippie in my heart and soul.

Cheech Marin, one-time half of the comedy team
Cheech and Chong

Over-thirty mothers giving birth for the first time have more than quadrupled since 1970.

According to the National Center for Health Statistics

A baby cost $5774 in its first year of life.
> *As reported by* AMERICAN DEMOGRAPHICS

Over half of men and more than two-thirds of women who get divorced are married before the age of 25.
> *According to demographers Teresa Castro-Martin*
> *and Larry L. Bumpass*

Fathers suffer from the empty nest syndrome as much as mothers when their last child leaves for college or to get married.
> *Professor Robert A. Lewis*

While the married-couple family still makes up the majority of American households, this number is declining, while the fastest growing segment of households are those headed by men and non-families—those living alone or with a non-relative.
> *Economist Kim Kennedy*

2.4 million couples wed, 1.16 million couples got divorced, and 4 million babies were born in 1989.
> *According to the National Center for Health Statistics*

He'll have a fairly stable future. Not one where the school-yard talk is whose father grossed $8 million on his last picture. I hope he'll grow up in New England somewhere. I want a more accessible lifestyle—for him and for us.
> *Michael J. Fox talking about his infant son*

The women [who marry millionaires] usually do everything for their men. They pack for them, make their phone calls and see if their drawers look nice. It's intoxicating for a man to be waited on. Combine this with very, very skillful sex, and that will get them.
> *Author Doris Lilly*

When I talk to them about drugs or any kind of stimulants, I advise them that the best thing to do is be straight and stay natural and don't use any drugs or stimulants or booze or anything.

Paul McCartney, talking about the advice he gives to his children about saying no to drugs

These satisfied couples yelled and did a lot of negative stuff, but in the midst of their anger, they somehow were able to express some positive feelings—of warmth, caring, even humor—as well. Even midway through a fight, when an argument is typically at its peak, these couples managed to talk about ways of solving the problem.

Pyschologist Gayla Margolin

The 1990s are going to be the decade of the couple. We'll see that relationships can't be taken for granted anymore.

Dr. Samuel Pauker

Studies show that 30 to 50% of couples are already abusive before marriage, either verbally or physically.

Howard Markman

It's stupid to be jealous of your partner's past. That's none of your business. I know Lisa had sex before we met. I can handle that. Of course, she didn't enjoy it.

Comedian Rick Reynolds

It's true no matter whether the kids have been good or bad, whether they are stepchildren or biological children, whether you're the mom or dad, what type of parenting role you've followed. When the last kid leaves home, the marriage improves. It may even experience a brief mini-honeymoon . . . [because] the two have more time together.

Sociologist Lynn White, giving the results of an eight-year study

We need a new model of adolescent development, one which makes sense of the continued love between child and parent.

Terri Apter in ALTERED LOVES: MOTHERS AND DAUGHTERS DURING ADOLESCENCE

"I'd be lost without you." "On the contrary," he replied,"I hope I'll have taught you how to live."

Author Laurie Graham reporting on her marriage to George Schieffelin, who was thirty years her senior, in REBUILDING THE HOUSE

My mother had an affair. It destroyed her marriage because she believed she had to choose. Not me! I love my husband and our life together. My affair supplements my marriage.

Anonymous, as quoted in COSMOPOLITAN

Intimacy involves many things; it is part of a wheel. You must have commitment, honesty, trust, empathy, sharing of events and time, caring about each other. It requires work.

Dr. William M. Chavis, Director for the Center for Sexual Health at Wayne State University

There's only a slight difference between keeping your chin up and sticking your neck out but its worth knowing.

CINCINNATI ENQUIRER

A woman who "marries up"—to a man better educated than she is—tends to live longer than one whose mate is her equal in education.

According to a study at the University of Michigan

[Marital] communication doesn't have to be spelled with a capital C; communication is talking about the ordinary things in life.

Author Francine Kalgsbrun

More than 2.4 million couples married last year. Only 64% of the total were first-marriage couples.

According to BRIDE'S MAGAZINE

Marriage has a lot of power in determining people's moods. It provides us with the social support needed to prevent depression. But a bad marriage can generate stress—a risk factor for depression.

Steven Beach

The five most popular months for marriage:
1. June
2. August
3. September
4. May
5. July

According to the National Center for Health Statistics

The father's concerns about child-rearing:
1. Finances
2. Health
3. Accidents
4. Discipline
5. Bringing them up right
6. Drugs
7. School performance

Mother's concerns:
1. Health
2. Accidents
3. Bringing them up right
4. Discipline
5. Drugs
6. Finances
7. Eating right

According to a study by Drs. Gunnard B. Stickler and
Daniel D. Breughton

Love is not being prettier or getting thinner; its about how another human being feels when he's in your presence. Tell him you love him at least three times a day, and compliment him at least once.

Author Ellen Kreidman

More than half of 72 couples reported declining satisfaction with their relationships during the two years after their first child was born, while only 20% said their marriage improved after starting a family.

According to a study by psychologists Carolyn Pape Cowan
and Phillip Cowan

Since [the couple] plan to spend the next two years in Japan teaching English, the couple neither want nor need a lot of household objects. So instead of registering a silver pattern at Tiffany's [they registered at Tower Records].

From the MARIN INDEPENDENT
JOURNAL

The average wedding cost is $13,310.

According to MODERN BRIDE

If someone invites you to sit through three hours of video-tape of their child, don't be a wimp. Politely put them in their place with a joke: "I'll look at your video of Suzie if you promise to watch five hours of my dog."

Letitia Baldridge

Whatever makes you happy makes you look good. That's why people look good when they're in love.

Fashion model Paulina Porizkova

Men who married in the 1960s waited an average of seven years before having their first affair; their wives waited 18. . For people married in the 1970s or later, a new "itch" has emerged: Men are faithful an average of five years; women only 4 1/2.

Georgia Wood-Leigh

Daddys don't just love their children now and then. It's a love without end. Amen.

From a song sung by George Strait

Divorced and widowed people in their 20s and 30s have particularly high risks of dying relative to married people of the same age—sometimes by a factor of 10.

According to a Princeton University study

EDUCATION

In a nationwide pole of 1,986 students, all with "A" or "B" averages, 54% graded the over-all quality of education at their schools a "B," 22% gave it a "C," and 20% an "A."

According to the WHO'S WHO AMONG AMERICAN HIGH SCHOOL STUDENTS twentieth annual survey

Our challenge lies in keeping children interested in reading by making it more fun and stimulating in libraries and at home. It is critical that we look for ways to maintain a child's early enthusiasm toward reading because we've seen a direct correlation between reading at young ages and a child's future ability to comprehend and learn.

Ann Weeks of the American Library Association

This greater career-orientation . . . is not really surprising. Today's young people, after all, may be the first generation of Americans unable to anticipate being better off than their parents. We have told them they have to compete more aggressively for a piece of a smaller pie.

Dan Sullivan, president of Allegheny College

Students do not appear to be focused on societal issues as in previous decades, although there is some interest in pollution, consumer rights, and disarmament. What appears to be especially important to students today is training and the ability to get a job.

Josephine Johnson, Western Illinois University

My sense is that today's students are service-oriented; many high school students are involved in developing groups or chapters against drunk driving. They will continue to struggle with balancing the pragmatic side of making a living with volunteerism and helping society.

Jim Skiff, Manhattanville College

The children of the 21st century will need viable adult role models who live by the principles they profess. They'll need to have a solid set of values, a basic trust in themselves, strong coping mechanisms, and high self-esteem to survive.

Prof. Povi Toussieng

The only industrial nation with a school year shorter than ours is Belgium with 160 days.

Educator Samuel G. Sava

AND SO FORTH

$82.5 million and $78.1 million.

The prices paid, within 48 hours, by Japanese paper manufacturing executive Ryoei Saito, for paintings by Van Gogh and Renoir

I used to do drugs. I got so wrecked one night, I waited for a stop sign to change—and it did.

Comedian Steve Krabitz

I thought about it, and I have run some figures, and I am afraid you'd make a very expensive husband.

From a cartoon by William Hamilton

My own adolescent rebellion came late. Somewhere around the age of 35. I don't recommend waiting till then. Better to drag your parents through it than your kids.

Author Judy Blume

Thirty-one percent of Nintendo users are adults.

Karen Beck, spokeswoman for Nintendo of America

The movie theatre was a cathedral where stars could be worshipped, but the TV in the living room brings them down to size and dispels the attitude that we should be polite to them.

Professor Mark Crispin

I do about 260 pizzas an hour.

America's champion pizzamaker, Waheed Azim

American children see 100,000 TV commercials for beer before they reach age 18, and usually take their first drink by age twelve.

According to studies cited by the National Council on Alcoholism

It tends to isolate you from the rest of the world. It is impossible to have [a conversation]. That's why you have to limit yourself, but it's difficult.

Michael Firestein, a 31-year-old Los Angeles lawyer, commenting on his Nintendo addiction

Lovely walled-in home of Pia Zadora. One-story city view estate with five bedrooms, 6 1/2 baths plus maid's bath. Large gourmet kitchen and media room, projection TV. Large living room, master bedroom with oversized glass doors, his/her baths of granite and honey onyx, custom closets, dressing areas and gym. Lush grounds and spa for the young at heart. Two-story guest house, four-car garage, security system and electric gated motor court.

Ad for the Beverly Hills home of Pia Zadora and husband Meshulam Riklis (price: $5.5 million)

I forgot my homework, Miss Houston. . . . After school I can fax it to you.

From the cartoon "What a Guy!" by Bill Hoest

The future is arriving on an express train, and it might arrive before we're ready.

Columnist Jack Anderson

There is only one thing better than making millions and that's spending them.

Robin Leach

If there is a single lesson from the '60s, it is the belief in our own capacities as individuals. We all matter.

Singer Peter Yarrow

Going to school in Palm Springs has its drawbacks. Tell me, where do you go for spring break?

> *Comedian Bob Hope at Palm Springs High School*
> *commencement*

The "Just Say No" campaign is extremely simplistic. It should be "Learn how to moderate your behavior. Learn how to resist the pressure to go overboard."

> *Brian Flay, director of drug prevention research at the*
> *University of Illinois, on findings that self-control may be*
> *more important than abstinence when it comes to using drugs*

My cars are so bad that when I want to stop, I don't need to use the brakes, I just put the air conditioner on.

> *Peter Fogel*

Having a baby is like living with a vampire. They sleep by day and suck the life out of you at night.

> *Bobbie Slayton*

Three things that people would like to see in restaurants:
1. Child care
2. Frequent diner bonuses
3. Call buttons on tables to summon waiters

> *From a survey reported on radio news*

Governor, the people of the Orange Coast are hurting. Their beaches are covered with oil—they don't need to get slimed again.

> *State Controller Gary Davis appealing to the California*
> *Governor to do something about the oil-drenched coast*
> *resulting from a crude oil spill*

Most people think to enter marriage with a contract is unromantic. Maybe I'm just a cynic . . . in second or third marriages everyone [should have a contract]. Life has become very complicated.

> *Iris Mitgang,* FAMILY LAW SPECIALIST

There is something grievously wrong with a culture that values Wall Street sharks above social workers, armament manufacturers above artists, or, for that matter, corporate lawyers above homemakers.

Barbara Ehrenreich

We're separating in order to retain our friendship.

Actress Dyan Cannon, on her change in marital status

In Orange County, California, freeway traffic reports are now a regular feature on the midnight radio newscast.

C. Kenneth Orski, President of Urban Mobility Corporation

Florida has ten vehicles for every ten human beings—more than any other state in the union . . . even car-crazy California with a mere 8.5 vehicles for every 10 people.

SAN FRANCISCO EXAMINER

You are probably not old until most of your friends have died.

*Response picked by 60% of respondents to a
poll on middle-age*

Chocolate [no longer vanilla] is America's favorite flavor.

According to a recent Gallup survey

Newly slim Fergie missed on her first outing . . . in a bright scarlet suit and matching hat that clashed horribly with her red hair. It made her look like a big lollipop.

W magazine

The top 5 snack choices:
  1. Fresh or canned fruit
  2. Chips
  3. Cookies
  4. Ice cream
  5. Popcorn

According to the Good Housekeeping Institute

The 1980s were characterized by a deep materialistic faith, and the age—the age of Reagan, Trump, and Cosby—was always busy counting things. The decade knew itself by what it cost, and calculated its happiness in market shares and rates of consumption.

HARPER'S magazine

2.2 million people are seriously hooked on cocaine—almost triple the 862,000 estimate made recently.

According to a Congressional survey

He's my kind of man—bribable.

J.R. Ewing of "Dallas"

"Colortag." A plastic tag that retailers attach to clothing. If the tag isn't removed properly, it will spray indelible ink on the goods.

Janet Lowenstein

I think one of the reasons Americans are so reluctant to carpool is that, for many, the commute is their Walden Pond—their only quiet time alone.

Anthropologist Katherine Sands

More than 20,000 kids participated in the Nintendo World Championships in Manhattan.

According to FORBES magazine

In addition to pizza, now at about 200 outlets, [McDonald's] is testing pasta dishes such as spaghetti and fettucini plus fish-and-chips in a few stores.

Lois Therrien

By encouraging critical thinking, we teach the student what we think is right, but we encourage the student to scrutinize our reasons and judge independently the rightness of our claims.

Harvey Siegel

The city is asking Domino's Pizza drivers to slow down and smell the garlic.

KQED news

In 1989 2.3 billion bottles of water were sold in the United States. In 1990 sales were expected to exceed 2.5 billion.

According to HEALTH

Nine ideas to improve the schools:
1. Deregulate teachers
2. Empower teachers
3. Let kids tutor each other
4. Use experts as co-teachers
5. Allow open enrollment
6. Diversify schools
7. Make schools smaller
8. Practice democracy in classrooms
9. Acknowledge individual learning styles

Mark Satin

[Children] see 25,000 television ads by the time they are seniors in high school. . . . Our leaders have exposed millions of children to a pattern of commercial exploitation that even shocks Western European merchants because they live in countries where children's ads on TV are banished since small children are not able to distinguish between programs and ads.

Ralph Nader

Some people prolong their unhappiness by dramatizing it, which is like expecting applause for having a headache.

Vernon Howard, QUOTE *magazine*

Fame and fortune ought to add up to something more than fame and fortune.

Robert Fulgham

. . . It's not a big mansion by today's standards. The bathrooms and closets are miniscule, and the upstairs of the main house is completely inadequate.

Los Angeles real estate broker commenting on the sale of the Beverly Hills mansion of the late movie mogul Jack Warner for $47.5 million to record magnate David Geffen

We're America's worst nightmare. White trash with money!

Tom Arnold, spouse of Roseanne Barr

Households whose incomes exceed $50,000 a year are 14% more likely than the average household to buy pistachio nuts.

According to data compiled by MediaMark Research

Its 37,000 square feet of living space will include a swimming pool, a trampoline, a library for 14,000 books, a game room, a movie theater, a beach, underground parking for 26 cars and a pavilion that will comfortably seat 100 for dinner.

PEOPLE magazine describing the new house of William Gates, software tycoon

Billionaires per country:
    U.S.—99
    Japan—40
    West Germany—38
    Canada—8
    United Kingdom, France, Hong Kong—7
    Italy, Taiwan, Saudi Arabia, Switzerland—6

According to FORBES

Almost 3 million American households are worth more than $1 million, but half of those depend on the value of their homes. When . . . the value of home equity [is subtracted], . . . only 1.5 million households can be classified as millionaires.

Blayne Cutler

More than 70 million Americans buy lottery tickets, but the people most likely to play are married, have kids, and live in the rustbelt.

Joe Schwartz

Eighteen percent of American adults have been asked to take part in a survey in the past year.

According to MARKET FACTS

About half of all Americans object to Styrofoam packaging for fast food and to nonreturnable glass beverage bottles.

Judith Waldrop

Those who eat the most hotdogs—at least one package a week—are blacks, women aged 25–44, those with school-aged children, and people who live in small towns and rural areas.

According to MediaMark Research

Fully 473,000 personal bankruptcies were filed in 1987, up from 241,000 in 1980.

Cheryl L. Russell

I have a problem saying that GI Joe is not good for kids, because he is a soldier. . . . There's a big difference between toys that use good-versus-evil themes and those that are violent.

Jody Levin of the Toy Manufacturers of America

SAT averages for the decade of the 1980s are up in 32 states and Washington, D.C.; down in 18 states. The largest gains were in D.C., Alabama, South Carolina, Louisiana; the largest drop in Washington state and Montana.

According to the College Board

The average adult makes eleven personal long-distance calls a month.

According to MediaMark Research

A funeral can be the third most expensive purchase a person makes, after a home and a car. The cost of traditional service with burial averaged $3,786 in 1989.

Consumer economist Mark Lino

After one's birthday, Mother's Day, Father's Day, Valentine's Day, and Easter are the most popular days for dining out.

According to RESTAURANTS U.S.A.

People in Des Moines used the *Yellow Pages* the most. New Yorkers used them the least.

According to a survey by Director Data

Shopping for food is another way of asserting control . . . a man might eat and experience a hunter-like feeling when he is shopping—like the primordial male coming home with the catch.

Professor Peter Stein on the notable increase in male food shopping

The average teenaged boy spends nearly $49 a week, while girls spend more than $55.

Judith Waldrop

Seventy-three percent of adults watch television between dinnertime and bedtime on weeknights; 59% of adults talk with other family members during the evening; only 34% spend time with their children.

According to a Roper report

The top five things that irritate drivers about how others drive:
1. Not using turn signals
2. Cutting off/pulling in front
3. Driving too slowly
4. Tailgating
5. Bad manners

According to a Valvoline poll

Things we can expect to see in the future:
1. A war between the generations
2. Skyscrapers more than a mile high
3. Mind-reading computers
4. A drop in street crimes
5. A decline in colleges and universities
6. Medical breakthroughs in the treatment of heart disease, cancer and strokes
7. All-plastic automobiles and airplanes

According to the World Future Society

More than three-fourths of the 60's generation believe that feminism, the willingness to question authority, and increased openness about sexuality are positive changes brought about by their generation. Eighty-one percent feel that more liberal attitudes on drugs and a greater tolerance of homosexuality has been bad.

According to a Gallup report

Fifty-two percent of all households own at least one cat or dog. American households now account for 57.9 million cats and 50.5 million dogs.

According to the Pet Food Institute

More Americans are eating out this year. Of those surveyed, 93% of young couples, 92% of young singles, and 92% of married couples working full-time dined out during the last week.

Economist Kim Kennedy

As the pace of life speeds up and people spend more time in the workplace, it affords them less time to spend on leisure activities. They are either "cocooning," staying at home using their VCR's, reading newspapers, playing electronic games, or just relaxing.

Professor Geoffrey Godbey

Quiet solitary time may facilitate relaxation and unwinding. Social withdrawal also allows someone who has been overloaded all day to avoid certain types of social stimuli at home that would further increase levels of emotional and physiological arousal.

Psychologist Rena L. Repetti

The "hot" items in grocery shopping: Poultry and fish, ice cream and frozen yogurt, health and beauty aids, delis.

According to the Neilsen Review of Grocery Store Trends

The top ten morning activities:
1. Personal hygiene
2. Listening to the radio
3. Drinking coffee
4. Making the bed
5. Making breakfast
6. Kissing spouse/partner
7. Reading the newspaper
8. Watching television
9. Exercising
10. Ironing clothes

According to a study commissioned by the
Robert Krups Company

[The elderly] get involved in fewer accidents than any age group. Though they comprise more than 11% of the population, they are involved in only 7% of all fatal accidents.

Tony Yanik of General Motors

The ten highways with the highest rate of traffic fatalities:
1. I-84 in Cassia, Idaho
2. I-25 in San Miguel, New Mexico
3. I-80 in Lyon, Nevada
4. I-15 in Clark, Idaho
5. I-10 in Pecos, Texas
6. I-10 in Grant, New Mexico
7. I-70 in Emery, Utah
8. I-10 in Reeves, Texas
9. I-59 in St. Tammany, Louisiana
10. I-59 in Lamar, Mississippi

According to a USA TODAY study

A parent's death is a major event in the lives of many middle-aged people. At the age of 40 or 50, many of the subjects said they felt like orphans. Coping with the death of an elderly parent may be one of the most important emotional tasks of midlife.

Professor Andrew Scharlach

Sexually abused young boys more often grow up to become abusers themselves than do girls who have suffered from this experience.

According to a study conducted by Professor Jan Gilgun

Another urban pet that's become increasingly popular in recent years is the domestic rabbit.

Richard Avanzino of the San Francisco SPCA

An extra hour of sleep helps people perform better.

According to a study conducted by psychologist
Timothy Roehrs

New punctuation marks generated for use in computer networks:

- (:-)   When humor is intended
- (;-)   A wink
- (:o)   Surprise or shock
- (:-(Sadness
- (:-/)   Sarcasm

James M. Coggins

Chapter 12

WORK

MANAGEMENT

By the mid-1990s, we'll define good management as the ability to get out of the way.

David Luther

Dismayed managers of Japan's Kentucky Fried Chicken franchises developed a unique strategy for attracting qualified help, offering new hires a trip to Hawaii.

C. S. Manegold

Make heroes out of employees who personify what you want to see in organization.

Paul Schumann

A meaningful management philosophy should provide answers to these questions: What does the company do for people? What does it do to people? How do people participate in the company's business activities?

Jack Falvey

When did I make my greatest hiring mistakes? When I put intelligence and energy ahead of morality.

W. Michael Blumenthal

In the ultimate time-management system, no one talks to anybody, because it takes too much time.

Jack Gordon

The job of a professional manager is not to like people. It is not to change people. It is to put their strengths to work.

Peter Drucker

According to researchers, at the 1000 biggest companies in America, less than 5 percent of the managers were women or minorities.

From a study by Korn/Ferry International and UCLA

Our study found that 58% of the nation's top CEO's joined their respective companies as their first job. Almost all the rest, 38%, had joined their companies at least by the time they had reached midcareer.

Professor Richard H. Dekmenjian

Among the 50 CEOs [in the top-grossing U.S. corporations], the average tenure in the top job was an impressively long 30 years.

Professor Richard H. Dekmenjian

The base salary for the average chief executive of a middle-market company (companies with annual revenues ranging from $1-50 million) in 1989 was $116,500. The average CEO also received a bonus equal to 49% of the base salary.

According to a survey by Ernst & Young

In choosing people for top positions, you have to try to make sure that they have a clear sense of what is right and wrong, a willingness to be truthful, the courage to say what they think and to do what they think is right, even if the politics mitigate against that. This is the quality that really should be at the top.

W. Michael Blumenthal

Only 39% of office workers believe that management is honest, upright and ethical, while 87% said it was very important for management to be that way.

From a Lou Harris & Associates poll

We will win only because we have better execution, not because there's this huge wall that keeps other people out of the industry. We knew that from Day One.

Thomas G. Stenberg, founder of Staples Office Supplies

Bosses are like diapers—full of shit and all over your ass.

Bumper sticker

Five fatal flaws of managers:
  1. Insensitivity
  2. Aloofness
  3. Betrayal of trust
  4. Over-managing
  5. Over-ambition

According to INDUSTRY WEEK

All good sales managers have teethmarks on their tongues.

Jack Falvey

Eighty-five percent of executives surveyed believe working over-time is not cost-effective. Most executives lose their energy and productivity after about ten straight hours of work.

According to BUSINESS MONTH

The majority of employers surveyed in the first four states to adopt parental-leave laws said "they were experiencing neither serious increases in cost . . . nor difficulty in administering and implementing the legislation."

According to the Families and Work Institute

Sixty percent of management women in large corporations identified a male-dominated corporate culture as an obstacle to women's success.

From a BUSINESS WEEK/Harris poll

Typical cost for hiring a new employee:
1. Executive—$6,076
2. Office-worker—$1,668
3. Production worker—$887

According to the Employment Management Association

Barriers to delivering excellent service according to managers and front line employees:
1. Inadequate communication between departments
2. Employees not adequately rewarded
3. Understaffing
4. Inadequate computer systems

According to Performance Research Associates

The most common perks offered to CEOs:
1. Company car
2. Supplemental life insurance
3. Club membership
4. Unreimbursed medical expenses
5. Supplemental disability insurance
6. Financial counseling

According to the 1990 OFFICER COMPENSATION REPORT

The dealmaker doesn't worry about the aftermath. A manager's whole life is the aftermath.

Richard D'Aveni, a professor at the Tuck Business School,
on why dealmakers make lousy managers

Appreciation is the most neglected—yet the most powerful—marketing tool available.

John R. Graham

The top ten CEO's and their total compensation:
1. Craig O. McCaw, McCaw Cellular, $53,944,000
2. Donald A. Pels, L.I.N. Broadcasting, $22,791,000

3. Jim P. Manzi, Lotus Development, $16,412,000
4. Paul B. Fireman, Reebok International, $14,606,000
5. Herbert J. Siegel, B.H.C. Communications, $13,702,000
6. James R. Moffett, Freeport-McMoRan, $13,517,000
7. Ronald K. Richey, Torchmark, $12,719,000
8. James Wood, Grade A&BT, $11,117,000
9. Roberto C. Goizueta, Coca Cola, $10,814,000
10. Michael D. Eisner, Walt Disney, $9,595,000

Management's top responsibility are: (1) providing motivation and leadership to employees, and (2) serving share-
holders.
According to a survey by Robert Half International

While the dealmaker thrives on immediate short-term wins,
the successful manager must be able to work in a more
ambiguous environment.
James Marks on why dealmakers make lousy managers

Negligent practices in hiring, retraining, and supervising
employees now represent three of the hottest issues in current employment law.
*According to Albert Zakarian and Joseph W. Ambash of the
Labor and Employment Group of Day, Barry & Howard*

[Gary] Hart, [Ivan] Boesky, and [Ollie] North have an over-
abundance of two of the three characteristics every leader
needs—ambition and technical competence, or expertise.
But they lack the third key characteristic—integrity. And
unless all three of these qualities are in balance, like the
legs of a tripod, a leader is bound to fail.
Warren Bennis, author of WHY LEADERS CAN'T LEAD LABOR

LABOR

Monitoring is a form of rape. They've taken everything off
of me and they can see everything.
Data entry operator on new methods of monitoring by computer

For many women, the comparable work plan [of the state of Washington] has simply reinforced segregation by sex. The typing pool, once a low-paid pink-collar ghetto, is now a better paid pink-collar ghetto.

Peter T. Kilborn

Women tend not to want to work with other women because . . . women are poor mentors, won't share, [and] are not as supportive as men.

Gioia Kay of the Center for Applied Psychology

Only 40% of working women polled in the early 1980s said companies should share the responsibility of day care, and the general public didn't want the Federal Government to spend any more money on day care. Today, 87% of the public feels there must be a joint effort between employers and the government to provide daycare.

From a report by the Communications Consortium

New teachers are entering the classroom as fast as the current group is leaving, which means the predicted teacher shortage isn't going to happen. . . . 28% have been hired in the past five years and 26% expect to leave.

According to a survey by the National Center for Education Information

The average male high school drop-out got a full-time job by age 22 in 1973; now he doesn't find a full-time job until he is 26.

According to economist Andrew M. Sum

The ultimate success of any compensation claim aimed at improving productivity rests on meaningful worker participation in the decision-making process.

According to PAYING FOR PRODUCTIVITY: A LOOK AT THE EVIDENCE

The 1.2 million Americans employed as private security guards earned a median $273 for a 35–40 hour week compared with $385 for all workers.

According to THE NEW YORK TIMES

Six million Americans work at home full-time. An additional 19 million work at home part-time.

According to L.I.N.K. Resources Corp.

Workers no longer think unions can deliver the gains in wages and benefits that made blue-collar members the world's best paid workers. For several years, union workers and private industry have been winning smaller wage increases than nonunion workers, and trade union membership as a part of the national work force has declined from 30% in the 1970s to 16.4% in 1989.

Peter T. Kilborn

Eighteen percent of working wives earn more than their husbands.

Journalist Jill Smolowe

Three-quarters of employees with children under age 18 handle family matters during work hours, and 40% of working parents miss at least one day of work every three months because they are tending to home affairs.

Blayne Cutler

The fastest growing jobs of the 1990s: Paralegals, medical assistants, home health aids, radiologic technologists and technicians, data processing equipment repairs.

According to the Bureau of Labor Statistics

A federal judge . . . ordered the giant accounting firm of Price, Waterhouse to award a partnership to a District woman it had rejected in the process that was biased against women.

Albert B. Crenshaw

Heart surgeons are the top earning doctors, while family physicians make the least. The average 1988 income for heart surgeons was $383,520, compared to $100,000 for general physicians.

According to a survey of 16,000 doctors

An estimated 71,428 people died from occupational illnesses in 1987 (the latest statistics available)—1.5 times more than auto-related fatalities. Among the factors contributing to work-related deaths: toxic chemicals, indoor air pollution, stress, repetitive tasks.

USA TODAY

The typical corporate meeting in America starts at 11 a.m., lasts an hour and a half, is attended by nine people, and follows a written agenda less than half the time.

According to a University of Southern California survey

As compared with productive, but non-innovative, members of the organization, [creative individuals] are likely to show a lack of respect for the way the organization traditionally does things. They're likely to be internally motivated, less receptive to authority, and less likely to stick to time tables.

Management expert Firdaus E. Udwadia

Most people can now look forward to 20 years of life after retirement.

Professor Rex Stith

The job characteristics that have become more important to young people:
1. A chance to earn a good deal of money
2. A job with high status and prestige
3. A job with good chances for advancement and promotion

According to Professors Richer Wasterlin and Eileen Crimmins

When people hear minimum wage, they think children working after school, and that's not the reality of it. The reality is that adults are trying to support families on this.

Joanne Mart of the Amalgamated Clothing and Textile Workers Union

You are not only workers. You are the men and women who are responsible for the health of the economy of this country.

Nelson Mandela to auto workers in Detroit

Most companies still are much more likely to give employees a parking space for a car than to provide a child-care slot for a son or daughter.

Congresswoman Patricia Schroeder

This is the hardest part about meeting a daily deadline . . . coming up with a good excuse for being late.

The professor in the comic strip "Shoe"

A new survey indicates a jump in interest in teaching, which got on hard times in the early 1980s after word got around that the only thing tougher than finding a teaching job was living on the salary. . . . Enrollment in the nation's teaching programs rose by 61% between 1985 and 1989.

From a study by the American Association of Colleges for Teacher Education

What is a non-essential government worker? I guess it would be any government worker who doesn't drive a snow plow.

From the comic strip "Shoe"

Total health care plan costs—including medical, dental, and vision care—rose 16.7% per worker in 1989. The cost per employee jumped to $2,748.00, compared to $2,354 in 1988.

According to A. Foster Higgins & Co.

What distinguishes the outstanding salesperson is this significant quality: Patience. The real pro knows when to be patient and willing to wait for the sale.

John R. Graham

22.6 is the average number of hours per week a working woman spends on housework and childcare. 7.4 is the number of hours her husband spends.

According to HEALTH MAGAZINE

Every builder of every home should be compelled to attach his name, in some permanent but inconspicuous way, to that house . . . for better or for worse.

Andy Rooney

Health insurance, dependent health care and a pension plan.

In that order, the benefits that attract job seekers

Videos get lifted wholesale, and the staff must be on constant patrol to keep drug dealers, often teenagers themselves, from preying on children. When the building closes, the librarian-baby-sitter must figure out what to do with very little kids whom no one has claimed.

New York Public Library librarians describing their jobs

United States wage growth will average 5.9% per year through 1991. The metropolitan areas with fastest wage growth will be (1) Boise, Idaho; (2) Albuquerque, New Mexico; (3) Anchorage, Alaska; (4) Norfolk, Virginia; (5) Burlington, Vermont; and (6) Baltimore, Maryland.

According to DRI/McGraw-Hill

Women quit their jobs because they believe they are on a dead-end career track and cannot advance any further, rather than because of conflicts between family and work.

According to a survey by Opinion Research Corporation

Lou was unable to take an afternoon nap after he retired until we got him that desk.

From a cartoon by E. Jole

One in twenty companies has an employee or employees with AIDS. Twenty percent of firms say their health insurance premiums went up by an average cost of 15% because of the AIDS problem.

According to the Executive Committee

Everyone's talking now about separating their garbage. Actually, I've been doing that for years. Only I call it "filing."

The professor from the comic strip "Shoe"

A requirement for every employee to take an annual vacation, during which someone else takes over his or her duties [can help to eliminate dishonesty]. Most frauds require a lot of day-to-day attention to keep from falling apart. An absence of even a day or two will undo everything. That loyal employee who never misses a day of work may in fact be ripping you off.

From THE NATION'S BUSINESS

Top salespeople are generally energetic, very much interested in the customer's wants and needs, highly time conscious, able to size up the probability of the sale quickly and accurately. They also set internal standards for their own performance, spend spare time in sales-related activities, follow-up with customers as promised, and put forth extra personal touches.

According to Thomas Rollins of The Hay Group

Among [pregnant] women who don't want to work, resentment toward their jobs may compound job stress, possibly leading to negative health effects. But if women want to work, the financial security and the emotional benefits of social support usually offset the bad effects of stressful work.

Dr. Charles J. Homer

Profile of a person at risk of the "Fast Track Blues": extraordinarily competent, exhilarated by control; called a whiz kid; driven to attain higher and higher goals (followed by a feeling of discontent); overworked; bedeviled by self-doubt; inclined to bend rules or lie to achieve goals; increasingly angry, moody and withdrawn; drinking or using drugs to get temporary relief.

According to Robert Bransom in COPING WITH THE
FAST TRACK BLUES

Interpersonal conflicts, especially those that occur at work, account for 80% of people's distress.

According to psychologist Niall Bolger

Throughout industry—because of exorbitant executive pay—morale is low and cynicism is high. Executives had better lookout!

INDUSTRY WEEK

The five best sales methods for attracting new customers:
1. Print advertising
2. Company catalog
3. Trade shows
4. Direct mail
5. Publicity/public relations

According to SALES & MARKETING DIGEST

The most new jobs in the 1990s will be in the service sector. Service employment is projected to grow 21% this decade. The fastest growing segments will be business and personal services, health care, and hospitality.

According to the Bureau of Labor Statistics

Of all employees who say their companies treat them with respect, 80% also say they are satisfied working there.

According to the Hay Group

Only 10% of private companies with ten or more employees offer any type of child-care assistance. Less than 1% provide child-care facilities.

According to the National Association of Working Women

Workplace sabotage is up and it's more dangerous than ever. With so much information sitting in computers, employees can wreak havoc by tampering with the data.
According to Professor Michael Crino of Clemson University

Moonlighters have higher self-esteem, are less anxious, are more practical, realistic and independent, but are less committed than other workers.
According to SAVVY

The most common employee benefits: paid vacation, hospital, medical or surgical, paid holidays, group life, paid funeral leave, paid sick days, paid jury leave, company-paid health premiums, long-term disability, dental insurance.
According to the National Institute of Business Management

For both sexes, the top source of stress on the job was a lack of information from above.
According to a survey conducted by Dr. Rhoda Green

What really works in marketing and sales:
1. Set a pre-call objective
2. Answer three questions for customers: Why listen? What's in it for me? Why buy now?
3. Ask for the sale.
Jack Falvey

The average secretary spends 118 hours a year at the copier.
From an ad from Minolta copiers

31.5 million Americans lack health insurance. An estimated one-half of the 31.5 million uninsured are under age 25. 11.7% of all Whites lack health insurance, 20.2% of Blacks and 26.5% of those of Hispanic origin.
According to the U.S. Census Bureau

Nurses spend more than half of their working hours on non-professional duties (answering phones, making beds, serving meals), only one-quarter of their time is devoted to caring for patients.

According to Benjamin Roundtree of the Hay Group

Forty-three percent of American workers are cynical, 41% are upbeat, and 16% are weary.

According to Professors Donald Kanter and Philip Mirvis

Men willing to work longer hours depend on their wives for way too much of th e work needed at home. Those not so willing get to pay for the privilege of having a family life. They pay in the coin of money and status and advances.

Donna Schaper and Warren Goldstein,
CHRISTIAN SCIENCE MONITOR

I have never met a policeman who is paid enough for what we expect him to do.

Commentator Paul Harvey

One hundred fifteen police officers were killed in the line of duty last year. Twice that many killed themselves!

Commentator Paul Harvey

Don't think of it as cleaning latrines. Think of it as an entry level position to the wonderful world of building maintenance.

From a cartoon by Mal

No one would ever surmise that teacher's work is crucial to the future of the country from the physical features of their work places.

Susan Moore Johnson in TEACHERS AT WORK

Sixty percent of women aged 35-64 have household incomes of $30,000 or more compared with only 40% of younger women and 25% of older women. Almost 70% of middle-aged women are employed, compared with 65% of younger women and only 20% of older women.

According to Simmons Market Research Bureau

The French *by law* work a standard week of 39 hours, get eight holidays and get 25.5 days of annual vacation. The Germans . . . work a 38 hour week, get ten holidays and have 30 days, 6 weeks, of paid vacation.

Columnist Michael Kinsley

More than 70% of the present jobs in America will not require a college education by the year 2000. These jobs form the backbone of our economy, and the productivity of workers in these jobs will make or break our economy in the future.

Former Labor Secretary Ray Marshall

U-Haul International, recently began docking $5.00 from the paychecks of its workers who smoke or are overweight. . . . Lost pay will be restored when personnel stop smoking or reach the weight level that U-Haul deems desirable.

According to PHILIP MORRIS MAGAZINE

The return of sweatshops—in the garment, jewelry and other light manufacturing industries—has resulted in thousands of children working along side their mothers in inner city basements and lofts.

Evelyn duBrow, Vice President of the Ladies Garment Workers

The share of the population in the paid labor force is greater today at 66% than ever before in our history.

Cheryl Russel

HOLLYWOOD

Doing a piece of acting is like making love to somebody. I say to myself . . . "Can I make love to this every day?"

Actor Alec Baldwin

If I didn't have children, I'd be a much better actress. I wouldn't be so distracted.

Actress Jessica Lange

When you approach acting when you're younger, it's about novelty and sex. It's about being attractive to your peers. You need an identity. As an adult, acting is different. It's much more serious. You have to be courageous.

Peter Horton, of "Thirtysomething"

It is strictly situational ethics in this business. If you don't shoot, you don't get paid.

Paparazzi Sirup Ramey

This is not a democracy. It's a queendom.

Roseanne Barr, to the staff of her TV show

One woman says she's Lucille Ball reincarnated and wants to play herself in the movie.

Executive producer Larry Thompson, on auditioning for the TV movie "Lucy and Desi"

They wanted me to do a public-service announcement: "Hi, I'm Johnny Depp. Stay in school and graduate. "I've been working for these people for four years. Don't they know I'm a drop-out?

Actor Johnny Depp

When I'm ready to stop [acting], you'll read about it in the obituaries.

Actress Jessica Tandy

I don't think that to become a star from playing Superman is an incredibly noteworthy achievement.

Actor Christopher Reeve

Acting is just a way of making a living, the family is life.

Oscar winning actor Denzel Washington

Once you become a movie star, people come to see "you." You don't have to act anymore. And, to me, that's a danger.

Actor Morgan Freeman

In high school I separated myself from all the games people
would play. A lot of my friends were getting their hearts
broken by their boyfriends. I didn't need that. I was the
weird one. Rather than going to parties, I worked on my
career.

Actress Madchen Amick

If you stick around long enough, your chance will come.

Actor Paul Winfield

The business has been taken over by low-life sluts.

Bette Midler, on Roseanne Barr and other female comedians

For an actress, aging becomes a problem only when you
stop liking yourself as a person. Fortunately, I still like me,
inside and out. Not in a vain way—I just feel good in my
skin.

Sophia Loren

Most of this business is so full of s—. People take it so
seriously. . . . I mean, film burns. You can light it on fire.

Johnny Depp

What blacks does Steven Spielberg know? Quincy Jones?
Michael Jackson? Maybe Prince? They aren't regular black
people.

Filmmaker Spike Lee

Everyone claims they're just happy to be nominated, but
they'd sell their families to win.

James Woods on the Oscars

An item in *The Tennessean* said New Kid wannabes should
play lead guitar; bass or piano, adding that "singing ability
is helpful but not essential."

Lisa Bernhard

I was 23, 25; I said, "What am I going to do when I'm 45?
I'm going to look so old. . . . I don't have any cheekbones.

I'm too round." And he said, "No, you have a face that will stay. The women with cheekbones won't." I thought he was just blowing smoke.

> *Goldie Hawn, 44, talking to* PEOPLE *magazine about how Warren Beatty predicted years ago that she would age well*

First of all, I think nepotism is great. Second of all, f—k them. I'm not too worried about what other people think. I think that in one of the truly nastiest industries, anything to get a leg up is good. . . . Without [nepotism] would we have had Jane Fonda, Laura Dern, or Matthew Broderick?

> *Actress Jenny Lumet*

I can't be funny if my feet don't feel right.

> *Comedian Billy Crystal tells* LIFE *magazine why he wears funny shoes for performances*

I was disappointed when she didn't get a part in *Dick Tracy.* Then I thought "What am I doing?" Pushing Farrah to do a movie with Warren Beatty, a man who likes to become lovers with his leading ladies. Why should we sacrifice our relationship so she could get a movie?

> *Ryan O'Neal, talking about the love of his life Farrah Fawcett*

You know, I've done 70 plays in my life, 28 movies and 39 TV shows and I think, "Couldn't I possibly at least get a salary that matches Tom Cruise's per diem?"

> *James Woods*

You don't photograph 32-year-old thighs in color. No, no, no.

> *Sharon Stone,* TOTAL RECALL *costar on why her recent* PLAYBOY *layout was in black and white*

Well, I'm just startin' to make it. I only own a Honda. And I have one lady who comes to clean in the mornings. But I'll never be like those a— holes in Beverly Hills, where after 30 minutes you're still drivin' in the guy's driveway.

> *Bob Hoskins*

Warren insisted that I get fatter. He wanted to pour me into my dresses. I gained 10 pounds. . . . I had to bleach my hair blond again, pluck my eyebrows. It was traumatic to get the hair right. Hair is the most important thing to Warren. He would walk around me like a vulture, making me feel like the ugliest thing in the world. And the dresses! We were at Western Costume, and he'd say, "Tighter, tighter, cut it down lower." I felt like a mannequin, a slab of beef. I was treated that way on the set—the lust factor.

> *Madonna, describing the pressures of playing Breathless Mahoney opposite "Dick Tracy" Warren Beatty, in* PREMIERE

He could get Mother Teresa to spit on him and walk off the show.

> *Comedian David Brenner, talking about radio's reigning king of shock jocks, Howard Stern*

I want to have a career like Spencer Tracy, Robert DeNiro, Gene Kelly, Omar Sharif. I want to do roles that have a positive impact. With the state the world is in, I'm looking for a hero.

> *Patrick Swayze talking to* PARADE

AND SO FORTH

I don't know that it makes any difference, but it's weird for your chief to be pregnant.

> *Houston Police Sergeant Robert Watson commenting on the pregnancy of Houston police chief Elizabeth M. Watson*

[The work-force crisis] pales in comparison with the management crisis. Workers work with the tools they are given. Workers do not reorganize the workplace. Managers do.

> *Former Labor Secretary William Brock*

I'm clearly not a major legal genius.

> *John F. Kennedy Jr., after flunking the bar exam for the second time*

It should not be noteworthy that I am a black, woman law school dean. Women should enjoy their successes, but we should strive for the day that the successes are so common that they become commonplace.

Marilyn Yarbrough, dean of the University of Tennessee College of Law in Knoxville

Unless the school considers non-Wasp candidates, Harvard's greatness is at an end.

Law professor Alan Dershowitz, on the search for a new president for Harvard University

According to recent studies, the attitudes of housewives are diverging from those of working women.

Cheryl Russel

It's conceivable that a painting wrapped in brown wrapper . . . well, it could have been taken out with the garbage.

Art Institute of Chicago director James Wood, on how the museum may have "lost" the $500,000 Georgia O'Keefe painting "East River From Shelton"

I once said that a good review stops me working for three days, a bad review stops me for four days. All you have to remember is that the pup is going to piss on the newspaper, and that everyone except yourself is going to forget [bad reviews].

Novelist Mary Lee Settle

As a member of the sex that purchases 40% of the automobiles in this country, I look forward to buying a car some day from a woman.

Sharon Nelton

Trust cannot be treated as if it were a medical plan. It has to be built up over time.

Harry Levinson

Bad service is the #1 reason why customers stop patronizing a business.

According to Harris M. Plotkin of Plotkin & Associates

Being an entrepreneur means blending the best of the tried-and-true business approaches with an element of experimentation.

CEO Rob E. Dalton

Casual users tell us they will stop using drugs if they have a reason to. You can affect a lot of people's behavior by hitting them in the paycheck.

William J. Bennett, Director of the Office of National Drug Control Policy, speaking to American business representatives

People say, "I'd love to own a store like this." Hey, you'd better love it so much that you're there fourteen hours a day, seven days a week.

Store owner Judy Watt

The mood of the 80s— Get what you can, can what you get, and sit on the can.

Congresswoman Pat Schroeder

It took me a long time to say m-m-m-marriage. Just uttering the word b-b-b-baby is difficult. . . . Career decisions are easier than personal decisions.

Newswoman Connie Chung

Today's family needs at least two paychecks just to maintain yesterday's standard of living.

John J. Sweeney, President of Service Employees International Union

I don't know how any woman can be a corporate officer or do any job all day and then come home and be a wonderful wife and mother. The 80s notion of having it all, being it all, has placed an enormous burden on women.

Actress Joanne Woodward

I wish I could say it was immaculate conception, but it wasn't.

> *South Dakota corrections official Lynne Delano, on 2 female prisoners who became pregnant*

Affirmative action is organized government racism against white people. . . . Individual merit should be the only criterion.

> *Michael Spletzer, co-founder of Temple University's White Student Union*

I strongly object . . . to the Federal government mandating leave policies for America's employers and work force.

> *President George Bush vetoing a bill that would have required larger employers to provide up to 12 weeks of unpaid family leave*

Former President Reagan will receive $1000 a minute for a one hour talk to 1400 owners of Hardee's franchises.

> *From the Associated Press*

Am told the dopesters can make crack in a microwave oven in ten seconds.

> *Journalist L. M. Boyd*

In an unprecedented negotiation, the producers of "The Cosby Show" have asked the National Broadcasting Co. for a $100 million "signing bonus" to renew the hit comedy for next season.

> *Journalist John Lippman*

Adults who think the "Made in America" is the most important indicator of quality: 25 to 45 year olds—8%; 65 and older—21%.

> *According to* LIFESTYLES

Chapter 13

SIGNS OF THE TIMES

BUMPER STICKERS

The bumper sticker . . . is secular America's *Book of Proverbs*.
John Shea

Not all women are fools, some are single
Bumper sticker

This car eats foreign cars
Bumper sticker

Hairdressers give the best blow jobs
Bumper sticker

Improve your image—be seen with mo
Bumper sticker

If we can risk nuclear war, we can risk disarmament
Bumper sticker

Midwifery is—a labor of love
Bumper sticker

The arms race has no winner

Bumper sticker

Test peace not nuclear weapons

Bumper sticker

War is costly. Peace is priceless

Bumper sticker

I prefer the Minneapple

Bumper sticker

Tree men get into more crotches than anyone

Bumper sticker

Home study students are in a class by themselves

Bumper sticker

Save elephants. Don't buy ivory

Bumper sticker World Life Fund

Duck hunters are a quack

Bumper sticker

The earth is our mother. Treat her with respect

Bumper sticker

Our taxes at work in El Salvador—70,000 dead!

Bumper sticker

Get in, sit down, shut up and hold on

Bumper sticker

I'd rather be driving my golf ball

Bumper sticker

If I'm driving irresponsibly, call my parents

Bumper sticker

My bumper sticker for [America's big ambition] would be that I want all kids in New Jersey and in the country to be healthy and educated, and to be able to look forward to a good job and a clean environment.

Senator Bill Bradley

T SHIRTS

T-shirt studies is an interactive discipline. It's up to the reader to extrapolate from individual Tees to construct a narrative out of textual fragments.

Brian Palmer

Y.U.C.K.E.E.—Young Unemployed College Kids with an Economic Emergency

T-Shirt

It's cool being black

From one of the pirated black Bart Simpson T-shirts

Dyslexics of the world untie

T shirt

Fergie Burger 100 percent fat

A British T-shirt

She's back and She's hungrier than hell

Karen Carpenter T shirt

Fax This

T shirt

LICENSE PLATES

Vanna YT

California license plate

Gngngon

California license plate

UGO2SLO

California license plate

Millionaire in training

License plate frame

Dare ya

License plate

Isabus

California license plate on a van

Amo SF

California license plate

MCH2 BSY

License plate

SECZME

License plate

Rlly-Hot

California license plate

IEO SLVR

Bumper sticker

OPRA GST

California license plate

IMSO FNY

California license plate

SIGNS

I shot an arrow into the air, and it stuck.

Graffito in Los Angeles, quoted by Robert Bryne

The Communist Party is bankrupt.

Sign at Leningrad election rally

Drug free school zone
Sign meaning any adult caught selling drugs within these zones may be sentenced to an extra 3–5 years in jail

No more yuppies.
Sign at the edge of town at Stinson Beach, California

LET MY PEOPLE GROW! STOP ABORTION NOW.
Sign at Right to Life rally in Washington, D.C.

How to Make Love to a Negro Without Getting Tired
Movie title

How to Make Love . . . Without Getting Tired
The way the preceding title was advertised in some newspapers

We know the truth. We believe the children.
Sign carried at parade after the exonerating McMartin child verdict

WARNING: May contain explicit lyrics advocating one or more of the following: suicide, incest, bestiality, sadomasochism, sexual activity in a violent context, murder, morbid violence, illegal use of drugs or alcohol.
From a bill passed by the Pennsylvania Senate calling for a label on records

Please abuse your drugs elsewhere.
Sign on the men's room door in a San Francisco bar

Drive-Up Divorce.
Sign in Salem, Oregon

I think! Therefore I vote Choice.
God is Pro Choice.
Signs at a Pro Choice rally

Helms equals death.
> *Sign at the San Francisco Gay Rights Parade*

Her Royal Highness the Duchess of York was safely delivered of a daughter at 7:58 p.m. today. Her Royal Highness and her child are well.
> *Notice posted on the railings at Buckingham Palace on March 23, 1990*

Bye, bye U.S.S.R.
> *Sign at rally for independence in Lithuanian*

PARENTAL ADVISORY: EXPLICIT LYRICS
> *Record company voluntary labels for records*

No this road don't lead to any God damn Russian duck.
> *Sign posted in Bolinas, California*

We cannot change unless we survive. We will not survive unless we change.
> *Poster*

PARTY 'TIL YOU PUKE
> *Daytona Beach marquee during spring break*

Things for Sale—Books. Condoms. News. Records. Mirrors. Hats, etc.
> *Sign outside a store called "Things for Sale"*

Life is a sexually transmitted disease.
> *Graffito spotted in New York City*

Will your child learn to multiply before she learns to subtract?
> *Children's Defense Fund anti-teen-pregnancy poster*

Kissing doesn't kill: Greed and indifference do.
> *AIDS-awareness poster proposed for the Chicago Transit System*

If you're not working on yourself, you're not working.

Poster

If we don't wake up soon, this place will look like the moon.

Poster

Reusable glow in the dark condoms

Sign over an adult bookstore

Feed our cities—starve the Pentagon.

Sign at a rally

CLASSIFIED ADS

Herpes—If you're an understanding lady with inner and outer qualities, style and values who enjoys fun and fine things, let's meet. Please be very slim. I'm 44, successful, Catholic and live in NJ.

Personal ad

SMOKERS!—Tired of Being Excluded? Meet that special person thru Smoking Singles—the monthly personals magazine. 6 issues—$10

Classified ad

Looking for Mr. Goodwrench—Woman, 43, pretty, weekend house, partial to Schubert, James Bond, hiking. Seeks man as handy with screwdriver as corkscrew, good-looking, funny, successful.

Personal ad

Call Your Mother—You've just found that nice Jewish boy she's always told you about. I live in . . .

Personal ad

Single Dad Wanted—Are you fortysomething, playful and passionate, smart and sexy? Me too. Do you have the world's best, brightest, most terrific children? I have two cats of similar description. Let's share.

Personal ad

Check-a-Mate. A service of Hill Street Investigations, Inc. Is he or she everything they claim to be? For Discreet, Inexpensive Background Investigations.

Classified ad

Condoms by mail. Avoid condom purchase anxiety syndrome (CPAS). Write for free color brochure.

Classified ad in HARPERS *magazine*

Living Proof—That not all the good men are taken. This tall, handsome, down-to-earth, never married achiever of 37 seeks a woman of warmth, honesty and beauty inside and out.

Personal ad

AND SO FORTH

The prestigious award was created and named for Michael Jackson in recognition of his humanitarian effort for all mankind.

The Los Angeles Area Boy Scouts of America Council presenting the Michael Jackson Good Scout Humanitarian Award

Feed the people, not the Pentagon

Bumper sticker

There was no question that I wanted a child. There was no question that I could raise a child. And there was definitely no question I hadn't met Mr. Right.

Jane Wallace, unmarried "Lifetime" talk-show host, on adopting a baby

He's her future ex-husband.

Anonymous

Recycle your motor oil; put a plastic bottle in your toilet tank; don't buy ivory.

A sampling from 50 SIMPLE THINGS YOU CAN DO TO SAVE THE EARTH

I've got more paternity suits than leisure suits. I feel very sorry for my wife. For her to put up with my nonsense, she has to be a very strong and wonderful person.

Engelbert Humperdinck

It looks like a beer. Smells like a beer. Tastes like a beer. Surprise. It's Buckler—non-alcoholic brew from Heineken.

Advertisement

John Sebastian is planning to join singer-songwriter Laura Nyro. . . . "Money from the concert will go toward a sanctuary in the Florida Keys to take abused dolphins and dolphins that have been stranded on the beach and rehabilitate them back to the sea."

Janie Coleman

Actually, I didn't go to this high school. I'm here just to meet some divorced chicks.

From a cartoon by Cohlsaat

Imagine what might happen if you walked into your boss's office and said something like, "Look, my spouse and I are eager to have children, so I'd like to cut back on my workload—but not my paycheck—so that we can spend more time at home having sex."

Chicago Sun-Times TV critic Daniel Ruth, on Connie Chung, who wants to cut down her workload so she and husband, Maury Povich, can try to have children

Euphemisms for disabled people: "The physically challenged," "the differently abled," and "the handi-capable."

Kate Anders Marlin

Control your urgin', be a virgin.
Pet your dog, not your date.

Teenage safe sex slogans

Dear Beth: I am seventeen and I have had sex with more guys than I care to count. I know how it feels to be impatient, like you've got to sleep with somebody, anybody, just so you can say you did it. I also know this: its not worth it! Sex with somebody you don't trust is an ordeal, nothing like the pleasurable experience sex should be.

Signed Wiser Now

It equals out. I pay alimony to Laurie and Denise, and I get alimony from Brenda and Suzanne.

From a cartoon by Sharris

My boyfriend's penis has a slight curve when erect. Is this common?

Question to COSMOPOLITAN

Warning when used as directed, cigarettes kill.

Anti-smoking advertisement

Talk is cheap until you call a lawyer.

From a button

New laws in Maryland, Connecticut, and Florida ban unsolicited facsimile transmissions. Eleven other states and the House of Representatives are also considering similar legislation against junk faxs.

According to BUSINESS MARKETING

$795

Value of an unused 1964 Kellogg's Cocoa Krispies box to a cereal box collector

I've got to admit smoking's not good for you, but neither is living in L.A.

Hervy Latour

TGIF&M
Commercial for F&M radio

Never, ever fax an invitation or an R.S.V.P. Just the thought makes my skin crawl.

Letitia Baldridge

If the plane starts to go down, I'm lighting one up.
Dave Noeth, on the ban on cigarette smoking in planes

Tossing tea
The practice of identifying anti-gay homosexuals, particularly those who are practicing politicians. Also called "outing"

Outing
The intentional exposure of secret gays by other gays

AT&T is not going to like me for this but I think using call-waiting is the most horrible, rude thing to do. I get really upset when someone calls me and gets me out of the bathtub to ask me a favor, then puts me on hold for three minutes.

Letitia Baldridge

Maintenance hole
New nonsexist name for "manhole" in Sacramento

My mother is terrified that I'll get married before I sow my wild oats.

Actress Molly Ringwald

Drug wars: America Fights Back
A new comic book about U.S. agents fighting drug lords around the globe

The age a child starts to use the microwave has become a bragging point with moms—like tying shoes and telling time.

Delia Hammock, Good Housekeeping Institute

The world isn't getting smaller. It's getting closer.
CBS commercial

If you want to be cool, stay in school.
The Council for Basic Education

Where there's Cos, there's effect
Sign advertising Bill Cosby's talents

Cap-Stun
A spray of cayenne pepper to deter attackers

Car Red. Knuckles White.
Toyota commercial

Is A.A.R.P. ready for Nancy?
Title of an article on the fact that comic strip character
Nancy became 50 years old in 1990

You are circumcised.
Translation from a Filipino banner at the San Jose Public
Library that was supposed to say "Welcome"

Today's successful comediennes are getting their laughs by joking about relationships. They're not bashing men or women, [as male comedians tend to do].
Donna Kaufman

Fit never felt so beautiful
Ad for Fruit of the Loom ladies' panties

The Politburo has reached a decision, Comrades . . . three Big Macs, two Quarterpounders . . .
From a cartoon by Dunagin

The —— from hell
Common 1990 expression

Simplesse
> *The name of the first low-calorie fat substitute approved by the Food and Drug Administration for the U.S. market.*

Try our new great gasoline—Super Unleaded With Oat Brand!
> *From a cartoon by Harris*

DIE NIGGER DIE
Written on floor of a black Emory University freshman's room

Hey Spic, if you and your kind can't handle the work here, don't blame the racial thing. . . . Why don't you just get out. We'd all be a lot happier.
> *Anonymous note slipped under the door of a freshman at Bryn Mawr*

Jew-Boy get out . . . I'm going to burn your Torah.
> *From a letter taped to a door at the University of Kansas*

And it wouldn't surprise me if Peter . . . will wind up in a paternity suit.
> *"The Bradys" producer Sherwood Schwartz discussing story lines for the revived series*

Cocaine lies:
You can't get addicted to cocaine.
C'mon, just once can't hurt you.
Sex with cocaine is amazing.
It'll make you feel great.
> *From an ad by Partnership for a Drug-Free America*

Save the world. If we're not all helping, we're all hurting.
> SPY

Honey
> *The most popular affectionate name lovers use according to a Korbel Survey*

To me he's more important than God.

> *A Columbian youth's evaluation of drug king pin,*
> *Pablo Escobar Gaviria*

There's too much money made by being Escobar's friend. And being his enemy is the quickest way to get killed.

A Western diplomat's evaluation of the drug war in Columbia

Teenage Mutant Ninja Turtles Cereal, Breakfast with Barbie, Hot Wheels, Nintendo Cereal Systems, Batman, The Real Ghostbusters.

The names of cereals that appeared on the shelves in the 1990s

Coke II

> *Proposed name for a new Coca-Cola*

Coke II will be directed at Pepsi drinkers. It will offer them two things: real cola taste plus the sweetness of Pepsi.

> *According to Coca-Cola spokesman Randy Donaldson*

Anagrams:
William Shatner—What man sillier?
Tom Cruise—i.e., Scrotum
Deborah Norville—O, her blond rival

> *From a selection that appears monthly in* SPY

Come on New York, ease up. Let's keep this the world's greatest city.

> *From an advertisement against rudeness in New York City*
> *by an organization called "New York Pride"*

You just say, "Are you prepared? Do you have one? Because, otherwise, it's no-go." If you are out of your own supply just say "There is an all-night pharmacy two blocks away. You can go get some."

> *Letitia Baldridge on condoms*

Nintendinitis.

> *Hand strain caused by too much rapid-fire button pushing*

150 Wooster

The name and address of Manhattan's most
chic restaurant

Bust this: Watch what I am doing.
Crib: House or apartment.
The Deuce: 42nd Street in New York City.
Five-o: Police.
Fly: Terrific.
Maxing: Relaxing comfortably.
New sack: New Kid.
Toy cop: School security officer.
Tweet: Teacher.
Puty: Student of a teacher who is no good.

Suicide is a permanent solution to a temporary problem.

From a suicide prevention hotline

Maybe I'm old-fashioned, but microwaving outdoors does
not feel like a barbecue!

From "The Better Half" by cartoonist Harris

Rap vocabulary:
    def: good, excellent
    dis: short for disrespect
    M.C.: rap talk for a rapper
    Skeezers: women
    stupid: good
    sweat: hassle
    the wild thing: sex

You probably aren't middle-age until you don't recognize
the names of the music groups on the radio.

Response chosen by 46% of respondents to a
poll on middle age

The Mary Leg Cross

What they call the way Mary Hart of "Entertainment
Tonight" crosses her legs (left over right)

Windshield tourists

> *National Park visitors who seldom leave their cars*
> *to enjoy the sights*

New leather your bound to love

> *From a marquee over an adult bookstore*

Chapter 14

FAR OUT

You know what they say about Marilyn Monroe: Every man in the world wanted her. And all they had to do was ask.

Geraldo Rivera

I can't stand nobody touching my toes. I have a real phobia about it. Like at night when I sleep, I have to have my toes sticking out from the sheet. I can't have them covered. That drives me berserk.

Roseanne Barr

Once I was to cross-examine a guy in a real estate deal, and before I was hired, the people told me, "We want you to cause him physical pain on the stand." I said, "Sure, okay, I can do that." And I did. He collapsed on the witness stand.

Lawyer J. Goldberg

As I was doing the cemetery scene, I kept imagining [my son] in that grave.

Sally Field, explaining her role as a grieving mother in "Steel Magnolias"

Undoubtedly, you will be familiar with some of our listings. But others—the International Veterinary Acupuncture Society, say, or the Center for Applied Intuition—may represent unexplored territory. You never know where some of these unusual resources will take you. We had a great time, for example, cooking up a vegetarian dog food taste test—with the help of *The Cookbook for People Who Love Animals* and three "animal-rights consultants."

The Editors of NEW AGE JOURNAL

You want to know the real [teenage/young adult] suicide statistics? They've gone down since 1977. This leads us to an inescapable conclusion. What were they listening to in '77? Disco. Disco killed more people than heavy metal ever will.

Frank Zappa, commenting on a court case involving suicide and heavy-metal music

I love animals and children. People I could do without.

Zsa Zsa Gabor

There were too many AIDS cases in the arts community.

Reason given by one insurer for denying insurance to internationally known cellist Paul Tobias and his wife

Most people know that they cannot contract [AIDS] by being seated at dinner with a carrier. But it is a courtesy to let them all know ahead of time.

Author Sidney Biddle Barrows

Everyone who is for abortion was at one time a feces [sic].

Peter Grace introducing Ronald Reagan, as quoted by Jim Angle on National Public Radio

If you continue this stupid fighting one more step, I shall give your sister and nieces a full statement that you committed a crime in helping your parents die. They will then be able to sue you for the $300,000 you inherited.

Message alleged to have been left on his estranged wife's answering machine by Derek Humphry, executive director and co-founder (with his estranged wife) of the Hemlock Society

Who doesn't feel a warm glow when identifying with the rich and famous? These are role models close to most American hearts.

Dr. Joyce Brothers

Women who complain about being deserted when their men take the afternoon off to look at a big game are making a mistake, for these same guys are likely to come away from the TV set feeling 10 feet tall and in dynamite physical shape even though, in reality, they've done nothing more strenuous than downing several bottles of beer and a hefty bag of potato chips.

Dr. Joyce Brothers

I believe all along most people are born with equal intelligence, but blacks have watered down their genes because the less intelligent ones are the ones that have the most children. They drop out of school early, do drugs and get pregnant.

Andy Rooney as quoted in an interview in THE ADVOCATE

I bet that women who keep their own names are less apt to keep their husbands.

Andy Rooney

I feel sorry for them [for homosexuals] more than anything. And I further offend them by feeling sorry for them, I guess. I think they got a bad deal, genetically. It's like being left-handed to the extent that the world makes it difficult for them. But I'm not Pat Buchanan, and [gay author] Merle Miller was a good friend of mine.

Andy Rooney apologizing for remarks that some have contended are anti-gay

The showdown in the Middle East is making a risky business even riskier for an exclusive group of high-stakes gamblers: those who insure companies against the perils of war. . . . Today's market: About $2 billion a year in premiums, covering more than $260 billion in potential losses.

Reporter Bill Montague

Senator Jesse Helms—Asshole men's jester.
Anagram by Andy Aaron

When people wanted his autograph or girls would come up to him, he could be quite rough with them. Twice he even took off his clothes at people—you know, pulled down his pants. What do you call it? Showed them his moon. I was mortified. But all of that is just to cover up how afraid he really is. He is so afraid of being hurt.
Sylvia Martins, talking about Richard Gere, her boyfriend for eight years

God would have been merciful if he had given him a little teeny penis so that he could get on with his life.
Actress Sean Young, on actor James Woods

I want to be the Shirley MacLaine of porno.
Pornographer Annie Sprinkle

I write about highs, like losing your virginity.
Martika at the 17th Annual American Music Awards

Drink it like a man.
Command by an adult as he handed 10 ounces of bourbon to 5-year-old Raymond Thomas Griffin, which subsequently killed him

The Vermont house is done now. And we bought an apartment in New York. We'll probably be based there and live in Vermont as much as we can. It's all part of the never-ending effort to keep life simple.
Actress Tracy Pollan

Most feminists aren't married, and have no children. . . . They are never going to get married because they can't find a husband. . . . I'm a normal woman.
Ivana Trump

"The Forbidden Dance" . . . tells of the story of a Brazilian princess who uses lambada dancing to save her country's rain forests.

Anita Snow, Associated Press

Drive-In Academy Award nomination for Viggo Mortensen, as Tex the Handsome, well-mannered cannibal in ["Leatherface: The Texas Chainsaw Massacre III"], the weirdo sex-fiend cannibal for throwing body parts into a swamp and saying, "Is it soup yet?"

Critic Joe Bob Briggs

We want to minimize as much as possible the impact on the lives of the people who live in Marin County—and at that hour, there's not that much traffic.

San Quentin Warden Daniel Vasquez, after a 3:00 a.m. execution time was set for the electrocution of Robert Alton Harris

I first saw [President Reagan] as a foot, highly polished brown cordovan wagging merrily on a hassock. I spyed it through the door. It was a beautiful foot, sleek. Such casual elegance and clean lines! But not a big foot, not formidable, may be a little . . . frail. I imagined cradling it in my arms, protecting it from unsmooth roads.

Peggy Noonan in her book, WHAT I SAW AT THE REVOLUTION

We came out of a very conservative time in the fifties. It was very stifling—Eisenhower, prepill. The only good part of it was that it was prepantyhose. I hate pantyhose. And prepill—you never got laid then.

Actor Dennis Hopper

Did you bump uglies with my sister?

Line from the movie TANGO AND CASH

Richard Pryor's son is a drag queen.

Title in the tabloid STAR

I say this a lot, and I probably shouldn't: the difference between rape and seduction is salesmanship.
> *Bill Carpenter, mayor of Independence, MO*

Because [Lolita Davidovich] has bigger boobs.
> *Actor Robert Wuhl on why he did not get the lead in the hit movie "Blaze"*

And that's what [golf] really needs . . . some striking female to take over and become the next superstar. It would have been Nancy Lopez, but Nancy turned to motherhood and so has her body.
> *CBS Sports producer, Frank Chirkinian*

I'm a killer. I can rip skin off a body.
> *Donald Trump's divorce lawyer, J. Goldberg*

Wheldone Rumproast IV
> *The name of Melvin Belli's dog*

I told him to take a picture of his testicles so he'd have something to remember them by if he ever took another shot like the last one. For you ladies, that's t-e-s-t-i-c-l-e-s.
> *Indiana University basketball coach Bobby Knight, when asked what he said animatedly to a player*

You can't be the President of the United States and also be a mother.
> *Barbara Bush*

The California Task Force To Promote Self-Esteem And Personal And Social Responsibility.
> *California State Commission created to help raise self-esteem in the state*

Elizabeth Taylor was asked how many husbands she's had. And she replied, "Mine or other people's?"
> *Anonymous*

For 1990 and beyond, I predict the dressing of pets as a tremendous fashion movement.

Fashion forecaster Bernie Ozer

Toad licking.

Fad, apparently popular in Australia, of licking slime off toads to get high

Sexuality upsets people, and women writing honestly about what they feel upsets people. . . . I think that I'm extremely lucky that I haven't had to go into hiding, like Salman Rushdie. I'm lucky they're not stoning me in the marketplace.

Author Erica Jong

When I did the last hit of smack, I already had Valium, heroin, cocaine, whiskey and beer in me. . . . I kinda remember waking up [and a paramedic] telling me I'd died, then been revived.

Nikki Sixx of Motley Crüe

I've been hooked on everything—dope, drink, sex—but I don't regret any of it. It was fun. I wish I could still do it.

73-year-old novelist Harold Robbins

I can't bear anything innocent being used. I think they should experiment on murderers. . . . Why not? They owe society something. Don't stand aghast at that. They're sitting there having three meals a day, and we're paying for it. What the hell are they going to do for society to pay us back? They should do that for us.

Actress Doris Day, on medical experimentation

The politician's spouse is usually a woman. Her role is to look adoringly at the politician when he talks and then to believe every lie he utters when he fails to get home at night.

Columnist Jimmy Breslin

I'll sit down with the little spike head, we'll straighten this thing out. There's nothing that a Catholic school, a paper route and a couple soap sandwiches wouldn't straighten out.

Drug czar William Bennett reacting to a Bart Simpson poster

I'm very compulsive about it. Toilet paper needs to be hung down along the wall. I'll actually rearrange it myself if I'm over at someone's home and I see it hung over the top.

Columnist Ann Landers

You can take the nigger out of the jungle but you can't take the jungle out of the nigger.

Phone message of a hate group in the San Francisco area

I looked at all the superstars. What is their different thing? Their hair. . . . I wanted to be a star. I said, "I have to fix my hair."

Rob Pilatus, of Milli Vanilli, on his $750 hairstyle

The 60-something Blackwell was paying $20,000 for a "complete face sculpturing," including cheekbone augmentation, eye restoration, silicone removal and regluing of his nose.

According to publicist Michael Sands

I am not the type of woman who goes to bed with every man at all. But if I meet a man, and I go to bed with him the first night, those relationships last.

Zsa Zsa Gabor

The Threat to the Cosmic Order: Psychological, Social and Health Implications of Richard Wagner's "Ring of the Nibelung."

Title of a two-day symposium at the University of California at San Francisco

Rock [Hudson] lived a life of incredible promiscuity. He had one, two, sometimes three lovers a night.

Producer Frank Konigsberg

What did Rock Hudson say when his doctors asked him how he got sick? "I don't know, you think I've got eyes in the back of my head?"

Author Peggy Noonan

What really causes marital abuse is more families. If all women had a lot of brothers, this would never take place.

Iowa State Representative Charles Percy as quoted by Anita Katz

Radical feminism, of course, has vowed to destroy the traditional family unit, hates motherhood, hates children for the most part, promotes lesbian activity.

Randall Terry, founder of the anti-abortion "Operation Rescue"

Sure, people pay money they may not owe. We make mistakes.

I.R.S. Commissioner Fred Goldberg, Jr. after a magazine report that the agency had erroneously billed taxpayers $7-15.3 billion

If he were here, I'd ask him if I could lick his eyeballs.

Christian Slater, actor and Jack Nicholson fan

Honey, maybe it's better that it's a boy because he'll be here to take care of you when I'm gone.

Sportscaster Frank Gifford to pregnant wife and talk show host Kathy Lee Gifford

It would seem from the interviews . . . that both of you have had few, if any, negative experiences when children yourselves, and also seem to enjoy a marital relationship where rows and arguments have no place.

Reason given to a couple in Leigh, England for denying them the right to adopt a child

I sport a caveman mentality. A woman should be a lady on your arm and a whore behind your door.

Nikki Sixx of heavy metal band Motley Crüe

If you stray, you will be shot.

A U.S. security agent to reporters waiting for the arrival of Mikhail Gorbachev

I've always maintained that there's a little bit of prostitute in all women. Or there should be. I think in order for a woman to be all that she hopes to be for a man, there has to be some of that there . . .

Actress Shirley Jones

Mom I'm on the horns of an enema.

Kelly on "Married . . . With Children"

I think you'd have to define what's meant by black. I have a so-called black neighbor two doors down from me who is lighter than I am. She told me for a fact that she's black, so you can't tell. We don't know about our club because we don't ask the members. There could be some with African or black blood.

Frank Rossi, president of Pennsylvania's Chester Valley Golf Club, on whether his club has any black members

A lot of times when you get popular you find you kind of make fun of your fans, and the more ardent they are, the more you laugh at them. Now I feel like you really have to cherish them.

Former rock guitarist Jane Wiedlin

I prefer girls who are young. When I eat a peach, I don't want it overripe. I want that peach when it's peaking.

Jim Brown, former football player

"L.A. Law" portrays its women lawyers realistically. In real life female attorneys tend to be overaggressive too. They generally lack a sense of humor; they're more defensive and have a misconception about what their male counter-parts do. I can have a real fight in a courtroom with a guy and then be laughing with him ten minutes later. With a man you don't carry a grudge down the hall. You can't do that with a woman attorney.

Marvin Mitchelson, an attorney who specializes in celebrity divorce suits

I'm not against the blacks, and a lot of the good blacks will attest to that.

Former Arizona governor Evan Mecham

The Air Force is paying $100,000 for a study to find out how much jet noise pregnant horses can stand.

According to the WASHINGTON TIMES

Come to think of it, why wait until May to visit Memphis? April is the month the Rev. Martin Luther King, Jr., was assassinated in the city.

From an item run in USA TODAY

You envy girls with beautiful bottoms? A ravishing, rounder derriere takes work.

COSMOPOLITAN

I think many American people have this clouded image of what normal America is about. Now it is very American for a son or a daughter to be a drug dealer or for the daughter to have a teenage pregnancy or abortion.

Actress Camille Cooper

Send dead roses. Dial 1-800-439-HATE and send someone "special" the gift they really deserve!

Advertisement in NEW YORK *magazine*

Charlie Chaplin used his ass better than any other actor. In all of his films his ass is practically the protagonist. For a comic the ass has incredible importance.

Italian actor Roberto Benigni

_____ your mother!

> *Tennis star John McEnroe to Ken Farrar supervisor of*
> *umpires at the Australian Open*

After you've played for three hours, I think it was unnecessary to disqualify me for a four-letter word. . . . I let things rattle me.

> *John McEnroe*

It's feminine, but important.

> *CNN fashion commentator talking about a fall collection by*
> *an Italian fashion designer*

When I'm with an ice princess or a bad girl, I can relate. . . . I've always wanted a woman who could really kick my ass.

> *Actor Nicholas Cage*

They're multi-purpose; not only do they put the clips on but they take them off.

> *Defense Supplier Pratt and Whitney defending the $999.20*
> *they charge the Air Force for a pair of pliers*

Air Crashes Getting Safer

> *News headline*

Relief Groups Help Hurt Family

> *ESCONDIDO TIMES ADVOCATE headline*

Multiple-personality Rapist Sentenced to Two Life Terms.

> *Headline for the GREENSBOROUGH NEWS & RECORD*

Retraction: The "Greek Special" is a huge 18-inch pizza and not a huge 18-inch penis, as . . . described in [an ad]. Blondie's Pizza would like to apologize for any confusion Friday's ad may have caused.

> *THE DAILY CALIFORNIAN*

Dimensional Foods Corp. of Boston has now developed a technique for stamping photosensitive molds on breakfast cereal so that you and your little ones can thrill at the sight of your favorite cartoon characters staring at you from the bottom of your cereal bowls in much the same manner as the holographic birds one sees on credit cards.

According to MEDICAL UPDATE

No, no. What if they were not as good as me? What would I do with those imbeciles?

Rudolf Nureyev telling Morley Safer why he had not had children

First World Congress on the Health Significance of Garlic & Garlic Constituents

Conference title

Canine Concepts, Inc. has just introduced "The Silencer," an electronic collar for dogs to control nuisance barking. It lets out a high frequency sound pulse in direct response to your dog's bark.

Unknown

"I used to idolize Liberace, but I'm so sick of sharing my house with his sissy ghost that I'm ready to burn the house down just to get rid of him!" moans the banker. "He's a real pest, prancing around here as if he owns the place. He's always re arranging my closets and throwing out my clothes because he says they're too boring."

A West German banker

Sometimes [they] don't smell too good, so love can have no nose.

Tammy Faye Bakker, in a sermon about the poor

To me one of the most exciting things in the world is being poor. Survival is such an exciting challenge.

Thomas Monaghan, the founder of Domino's Pizza

He does the most fabulous tongue tricks you've ever seen. Amazing ones. Like, he can make animals and shapes with it. I sat there for half an hour, and he did them for me.

Laura Dern on actor Willem Dafoe

I like East Coast people because they don't take crap from anybody. I think people on the East Coast read, too. Most people don't. And people on the East Coast generally have a bad attitude about things. I'm like that.

Roseanne Barr

. . . When you read a tabloid, your IQ plummets, you get a Southern accent, your butt drops, that's how stupid you become.

Roseanne Barr

Whenever I play, it should be an event. I'm a legend, and I should keep it that way.

Little Richard

Every once in a while I wake up and go, "My God, I was married once. I was married, and he was the love of my life." It is like a death to deal with.

Madonna, on ex-husband Sean Penn

She's the ultimate woman. She is a sex goddess and yes she is my whore, and she has been an inspiration. But marriage is something you still got to work at.

Singer David Coverdale

So many of Mexico City's 20 million people live without sanitary facilities that "fecal" snow often falls over the city as winds pick up dried excrement.

Susan Reed

I recall the very first day I ever spoke to a black kid on the air. I was terrified, because I didn't know what the reaction was going to be. I ran backstage to see if there was any reaction. And the wonderful irony was, nobody called.

Dick Clark talking about the first time that blacks appeared on "American Bandstand"

Ivan F. Boesky testified. . . that he had deducted from his taxes half of the $100 million he paid to settle insider trading charges, kept millions in ill-gotten gains and illegally bribed fellow prisoners to do his laundry.

Kurt Ichenwald

My breasts are beautiful, and I gotta tell you, they've gotten a lot of attention for what is relatively short screen time. I make no excuses and have no regrets for my past work in films. . . . And if my breasts have become the topic of dinner conversation at frat houses, God bless 'em.

Actress Jamie Lee Curtis, who, despite recent critical praise for her acting, is still better known for taking her shirt off in the 1983 film "Trading Places"

Anyone who's lived his life to the fullest extent has a scandal buried somewhere. And anybody who doesn't . . . I have no interest in meeting. . . . You show me somebody who'd led a perfect life, I'll show you a dullard.

Rob Lowe

. . . You know this for a fact—women in private are much filthier than guys.

Andrew Dice Clay, comedian, about why a large number of his fans are women

So I say to the bitch, "Lose the bra—or I'll cut ya." Is that a wrong attitude?

Comedian Andrew Dice Clay

What do I need—more P.R.? I couldn't get more P.R. if I took out my penis and wrapped it around a microphone stand.

Comedian Andrew Dice Clay

[Andrew Dice] Clay is saying the taboo words we don't dare use. That's why he's popular. He's telling the secrets we keep inside us.

English professor Leonard R.N. Ashley

Drexel Burnham Lambert Inc. paid some top executives bonuses of more than $10 million just weeks before its parent company filed for bankruptcy protection.

Associated Press

A lot of the guys said it was fate that stopped it. Probably I would have been dead if it went over.

Daredevil Dave Munday, whose foam-padded barrel got caught on a rocky shelf about a foot from the brink of Niagara Falls

[Most people] when given a choice between true quality and garbage . . . are likely to head for garbage.

Entertainer Steve Allen talking about what Americans like to watch on television

Americans believe that where there is a problem, there's always a solution. In Eastern Europe it's the other way around: where there's no solution, there's a problem.

Miklos Vamos, a Hungarian writer

There really wasn't much I was going to do about it. I made breakfast.

Angela Bowie, David Bowie's ex-wife, on allegedly finding the rock star in bed with fellow rocker Mick Jagger

The pain of birth actually prepares you for the agony of being a parent.

From the situation comedy "Grand"

Kimberly didn't want me in the delivery room. And I didn't really want to be there. She just felt it was a time of embarrassment. She is a very private person. [Witnessing the delivery] is not a mental image that I want to carry with me—I'm a very romantic guy. The support that I supplied was emotional.

Hugh Hefner talking about the delivery of his son,
Marsten Glen

What do you think about renaming the national anthem to the Barr strangle banner.

Anonymous

I want him to appreciate what they do for him. I find that a lot of children in Hollywood and Beverly Hills are not so nice to the help. We won't put up with that.

Kimberly Hefner, wife of Hugh, on how they will raise
their newborn son

Everybody got it wrong. I said I was into porn again—not born again.

Rocker Billy Idol, in PUNCH *magazine, refuting reports that*
his motorcycle wreck led him to God

Being traditional is not what made Kathie Lee take her husband's name. Being an opportunist is more like it. After all, there isn't much call for a gospel singer named Kathie Lee Epstein, and it was dating and subsequently marrying Frank Gifford that. . . put her into the limelight (her favorite place to be). What I'll never understand is how a once classy guy like Frank Gifford ever got involved with a fraud like her in the first place.

Jill Newton

Banned in the U.S.A.

Title of a new song by 2 Live Crew

[Rap music] is not something you have to be afraid of. It's a form of social commentary that is not different from other cultural expressions that have come from other generations of black people.

Dr. Walter Allen, Professor of Sociology of U.C.L.A.

[Rap] music represents how a particular group of young
black people—particularly inner-city young people—see the
world and their place in it.

Dr. Walter Allen, professor of sociology at U.C.L.A.

I'm the type of guy that eats it
When he wants and licks you
In places that your boyfriend
Dont.
You're the type of guy who will
Call me a punk, not knowing
That your main girl is biting
My chunk.

Words from "I'm That Type of Guy" by L.L. Cool J

How many ladies
Are deep enough
To handle a man
Like me?

From "All Night Long" by Kool Moe Dee

Wine is fine but whiskey's quicker
Suicide is slow with liquor. . .
Suicide is the only way out.
Don't you know what it's really about?

From the song, "Suicide Solution," by Ozzy Osbourne,
denounced by New York's John Cardinal O'Connor

Police and niggers, that's right, get outta my way.
Don't need to buy none of your gold chains today. . .
Immigrants and faggots, they make no sense to me.
They come to our country and think they'll do as they please,
Like start some mini-Iran, or spread some f——g disease.
They talk so many goddam ways, it's all Greek to me.

From "One in a Million," by heavy metal rock group
Guns N' Roses

Panties 'round your knees
With your ass in debris
Doin' that grind with a push and squeeze
Tied up, tied down, up against the wall.

From a song by Guns N' Roses

Laid out cold
Now we're both alone,
But killing you helped me keep you home.

From "You're All I Need" by rock group Motley Crüe

Ice Cube will swarm
On any m—— f—— in a blue uniform . . .
A young nigger on the warpath,
And when I finish it's gonna be a bloodbath.

From "F——Tha Police" by rock group N.W.A.
[Niggers With Attitude]

Why declare obscene 2 Live Crew, whose members are black,
and not Andrew Dice Clay who is white and whose frequently raunchy albums sit side by side to 2 Live Crew in
some stores.

Journalist Robert Hilburn

Index

Aaron, Andy, 280
Aburdene, Patricia, 104
Abzug, Bella, 18
Achtemeier, Elizabeth, 195
Acosta, Prof. R. Vivian, 156
Adkins, Larry, 94
A. Foster Higgins & Co., 247
Agnos, Art, 68
Alan Guttmacher Institute, 61, 121
Aleona, Rev. Ms. Morey Y. J., 192
Alexander, Karen, 20
Alexander, Shana, 19
Alexis, Kim, 217
Al-kandry, Mrs., 87
Allen, Dr. Walter, 293, 294
Allen, Nancy, 179
Allen, Steve, 292
Allen, Woody, 28
Alter, Jonathan, 83
Ambash, Joseph W., 243
American Association of Colleges for
  Teacher Education, 247
American Board of Family Practice,
  216
American Chemical Society, 206
American College of Emergency
  Physicians, 131
American Demographics, 53, 175, 221
American Heart Association, 109
American Medical Association, 115
American Society of Plastic and
  Reconstructive Surgeons, 126-27
Amick, Madchen, 255
Anderson, Dr. Robert A. Jr., 117
Anderson, Jack, 228
Anderson, Lauri, 219
Anderson, Robert Page, 59
Anderson, Sulome, 24
Annas, George, 123
Apple, Gary, 55, 88, 99
Apter, Terri, 222
Arnold, Tom, 10, 233

Ashley, Leonard R. N., 292
Aslund, Anders, 81-82
Asner, Ed, 94
Associated Press, 52, 87, 200, 260, 292
Association of American Physicians
  and Surgeons, 122-23
Atwater, P.M.H., 30
Automobile magazine, 211
Avorn, Dr. Jerry, 113
Azim, Waheed, 227

Baehren, Dr. David F., 134
Baker, Anita, 100
Baker, Russell, 24
Baker, Tammy Faye, 289
Bakos, Susan Crain, 215
Baldridge, Letitia, 225, 271, 274
Baldwin, Alec, 253
Baloo, 45
Bunking Safety Digest, 102-3
Barco, Virgilio, 88
Bardot, Brigitte, 25, 48
Barlow, David, 160
Barna Research Group, 192
Barnet, Richard J., 150
Barr, Browne, 32
Barrett, David, 197
Barrows, Sydney Biddle, 126, 278
Barr, Roseanne, 10, 33, 145, 146, 171,
  254, 277, 290
Barry, Christopher, 13
Barry, Dave, 126, 132
Barry, Marion, 12-13
Barrymore, Drew, 23
Bauer, Gary, 25
Bayless, Skip, 165
Beach, Steven, 223
Beatty, Warren, 10, 179, 181, 185
Becker, Teresa M., 184
Beck, Karen, 227
Bednarik, Chuck, 154

297

Shepherd, Cybill, 31, 32
Sheppard, R. Z., 209
Sheridan, Danny, 157
Shevardnadze, Edward, 82
Siegel, Harvey, 231
Siemens, Jochen, 77
Sigelbaum, Harvey C., 126
Silber, John, 30
Silensky, Richard, 36
Silis, C. J., 102
Silvers, Sarah, 132
Simmons, Gene, 193
Simmons Market Research Bureau, 252
Simon, Julian L., 70
Simpson, Alan, 42
Simpson, Carol, 59
"Simpsons, The," 172-73
Sinden, Harry, 156
Sixx, Nikki, 283, 286
Skelton, Red, 30
Skiff, Jim, 226
Skolnick, Jerome H., 66
Slansky, Paul, 18
Slater, Christian, 285
Slayton, Bobbie, 229
Sloan, Alfred, 103
Smalley, Rick, 207
Smeal, Eleanor, 49
"Smith, Adam," 19
Smith, Curt, 125
Smith, Jaclyn, 103
Smith, Liz, 6, 185
Smith, Ronald C., 144
Smith, Timothy L., 199
Smith, Tom W., 213
Smolowe, Jill, 245
Snow, Anita, 281
Sobel, David, 36
Sokolof, Phil, 109
Solove, Ronald L., 178
Soloway, Ann, 128
Soporowski, Joseph J., 128
Sorel, Louise, 180
Sorvino, Paul, 10, 185
Spackey, Lori A., 69
Spaeth, Anthony, 47
Speltzer, Michael, 260
Spencer, David, 203
Spero, Robert, 89
Speth, Gustave, 123
Spherris, Penelope, 175
Spiegel, Dr. David, 129

Spitz, Mark, 164
Sport, 154, 158, 159-60, 162, 163-64, 166
Sporting News, 158
Sprinkle, Annie, 280
Spy magazine, 274
Stacks, John F., 11
Stallone, Sylvester, 23, 179
Stanford University Medical Center, 113
Stangel, Chris, 3
Star, 281
Starzl, Dr. Thomas, 135
Stayskal, 115
Steinbrenner, George, 165
Stein, Prof. Peter, 235
Stenberg, Thomas G., 241
Stern, George, 17
Stevens, John Paul, 67
Stevenson, 4
Stickler, Dr. Gunnard B., 128, 170, 224
Stiles, Steve, 217
Sting, 174
Stipe, Michael, 175
Stith, Prof. Rex, 246
Stoll, David, 192
Stone, Sharon, 256
Stout, Dr. James, 64
Stoyle, Rosemary, 17, 141
Strait, George, 225
St. Laurent, Jeff, 207
Stromme, Jason, 184
Stutman, Robert M., 23, 66
Styron, William, 125, 138
Sullivan, Dan, 226
Sullivan, Kathleen, 31
Sullivan, Neil J., 155
Sum, Andrew M., 244
Sunlin, Mark, 207
Sunshine Magazine, 126
Sununu, John, 31, 34
Swayze, Patrick, 180, 257
Sweeney, John J., 259
Sweet-Jemmott, Dr. Loretta, 214
Szulc, Tad, 149

Talbott, Strobe, 70
Tandy, Jessica, 254
Tanenbaum, Rabbi Marc H., 194
Tax Foundation, 44, 61
Taylor, Elizabeth, 20, 179
Taylor, Gertie, 74